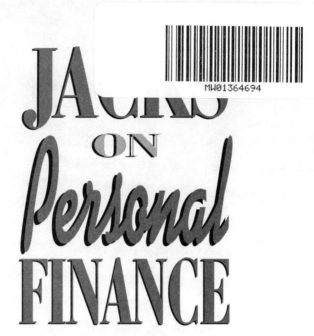

**Modern Money Management
for Utterly Confused Canadians**

JACKS ON *Personal* FINANCE

Modern Money Management for Utterly Confused Canadians

EVELYN JACKS

McGraw-Hill Ryerson
Toronto   Montreal

Jacks on Personal Finance: Money Management for Utterly Confused Canadians

Copyright © 1995 by Evelyn Jacks. All rights reserved. No part of this publication may be reproduced or transmitted in any form or by any means, or stored in a data base or retrieval system, without the prior written permission of McGraw-Hill Ryerson Limited.

Care has been taken to trace ownership of copyright material contained in this text. The publisher will gratefully accept any information that will enable them to rectify any reference or credit in subsequent printings.

First published in 1995 by
McGraw-Hill Ryerson Limited
300 Water Street
Whitby, Ontario, L1N 9B6

ISBN 0-07-551870-8

1 2 3 4 5 6 7 8 9 0 MD 4 3 2 1 0 9 8 7 6 5

Printed and bound in Canada

Canadian Cataloguing in Publication Data

Jacks, Evelyn, 1955-
   Jacks on personal finance

ISBN 0-07-551870-8

1. Finance, Personal. 2. Financial security.
3. Investments. I. Title

HG179.J3 1994   332.024   C94-932610-0

DISCLAIMER

This book is designed to provide accurate and authoritative information on the subject matter. It has been carefully researched and verified for accuracy; however, due to the complexity of the subject matter, and the continual changes occurring in the subject matter, neither the author nor the publisher can be held responsible for errors or omissions, or consequences of any actions resulting from information in this book. Examples discussed are intended as general guidelines only.

This book is sold with the understanding that neither the author nor the publisher is engaged in rendering legal, accounting or other professional advice or opinions. If such advice or opinions are required, the reader is urged to seek the services of a competent and experienced professional.

PUBLISHER: Donald S. Broad
COVER DESIGN: Dave Hader/Studio Conceptions
EDITORIAL SERVICES: Word Guild, and Marsh Hill Publishing Services
TEXT DESIGN AND PAGE COMPOSITION: Marsh Hill Publishing Services

Evelyn Jacks' hair by Suzy's, The Hair Professionals, Winnipeg, Manitoba

Evelyn Jacks' suit furnished by Danier

For Kathy and Salvatore

*The creation of a new life is simply
not comparable
to anything else you'll ever do.
It is the ultimate achievement.*

For Cory and Don

*My ultimate achievements,
I hope you find this book valuable*

Other books by Evelyn Jacks

Jacks on Tax Savings—11th Edition.
How to prepare your personal income tax return.

Jacks' Tax Tips—2nd Edition.
How to save money on your taxes all year long.

Jacks on GST.
Understanding how the GST works.

About The Jacks Institute

Evelyn Jacks is president and owner of The Jacks Institute, a private career college which specializes in certificate income tax preparation courses for individuals and tax professionals. Both manual and computer applications are taught in self-study formats. Individuals, professional tax practices and educational institutes across Canada offer income tax courses by Canada's Leading Trainer of Tax Industry Professionals—The Jacks Institute. To find out more, call 1-800-563-EARN. An information package is available, at no charge or obligation.

Preface

Jacks on Personal Finance is a logical addition to the *Jacks on Tax* series of books. Tax planning and money management go hand in hand. It is what you do with your money throughout the year that will determine how much tax you pay and how many "after-tax" dollars you will keep for yourself and your family.

At the outset, I wish to say that I am an educator, the owner of a private career college, a tax consultant and a writer. I am not a lawyer, stock broker, banker or salesperson of financial instruments. I specialize in explaining complex subjects to average people in plain English and in a format that is useful to the reader. Your financial professionals will help you choose the best products for your specific needs. Our goal is to present the many and varied options you may wish to follow in making the right financial decisions for your family.

I would like to acknowledge and thank the industry professionals who have assisted in verifying specific information discussed in this book:

Mr. Guy Bieber, Vice President and Sales Manager, Nesbitt Burns, Winnipeg.

Mr. Keith Carter, Senior Vice President and Director, Moss Lawson, Winnipeg, Manitoba—Financial Instruments.

Canada Bond Rating Service/Dominion Bond Rating Service.

Mr. Alan Lesperance, Lesperance Insurance, Winnipeg, Manitoba—Life Insurance Rates and Profiles.

Mr. Roper John McDiarmid, Montrose Financial Group, Winnipeg, Manitoba—Mortgage Amortization Schedules.

National Trust, Winnipeg, Manitoba—Mortgage Amortization.

The Paul Revere Insurance Co. for statistics regarding Disability Insurance.

Mr. Harry Schimke, Royal LePage, Winnipeg, Manitoba—Mortgage Insurance, Mortgage Pre-Payment Schedule.

Loring Ward, Winnipeg, Manitoba—Financial Portfolios.

Mr. Gord Wimble, Vice President and Branch Manager, Wood Gundy, Winnipeg, Manitoba—Risk and Reward.

Professor Larry A. Wood, Faculty of Management, University of Calgary—Mathematics of Finance.

Your accounting, legal, insurance, real estate and investment professionals are trained to provide you with the specific information you need about the financial products you wish to acquire and alert you to the planning required to maximize your investments. Shop around for the person you feel most comfortable with. These are important long-term relationships that will help you build your financial legacy.

I hope that this book will be valuable to you in managing your time and money in the 1990s and beyond. I wish you every success in managing your resources in the challenging years ahead.

Evelyn Jacks

Contents

Introduction		xi
PART 1	**TOOLS FOR ESTABLISHING A MONEY MANAGEMENT PLAN**	**1**
Chapter 1	Initiating Change	2
Chapter 2	Effective Decision-Making	4
Chapter 3	Your Personal Mission Statement	6
Chapter 4	Documenting Your Net Worth	8
Chapter 5	Charting Your Current Cash Flow	12
Chapter 6	Establishing Direction	15
Chapter 7	Implementing Objectives and Tracking Results	20
Chapter 8	Analyzing Results	22
Chapter 9	Budgeting for Success	27
Chapter 10	A Format for Budgeting	28
Chapter 11	Reconciling the Bank	33
Chapter 12	Fine-Tuning Your Results	34
PART 2	**OPTIONS FOR PUTTING YOUR MONEY TO WORK**	**39**
Chapter 13	Putting Your Dollars to Work	40
Chapter 14	The Relationship between Time and Money	42
Chapter 15	Entry into the Capital Marketplace	46
Chapter 16	Risk and Reward	49
Chapter 17	Debt Securities	53
Chapter 18	The Stock Market	58
Chapter 19	Common Stock	62
Chapter 20	What to Look For in Acquiring Common Stock	65
Chapter 21	Preferred Shares	70
Chapter 22	Mutual Funds and Other "Managed Money"	72
Chapter 23	Real Estate	73
Chapter 24	Your Portfolio Mix	80
Chapter 25	Protecting Your Purchasing Power	86
PART 3	**THE TAX SLANT**	**89**
Chapter 26	The Warm-Up Routine	90
Chapter 27	How Income Is Taxed in Canada	95
Chapter 28	Canada's Tax Rates	97
Chapter 29	What a Difference a Move Can Make!	99
Chapter 30	The Basics of Tax Planning	102
Chapter 31	Income Splitting	107

Chapter 32	How Interest Income Is Taxed	110
Chapter 33	Interest Deductibility	115
Chapter 34	Taxation of Dividend Income	117
Chapter 35	Capital Gains and Losses	120
Chapter 36	Special Rules When Things Go Wrong	127
Chapter 37	Inside or Outside an RRSP	130
Chapter 38	Spousal RRSPs	135
Chapter 39	Revenue Properties	137
Chapter 40	The Capital Gains Deduction	141
PART 4	**LIFE CYCLES: BUILDING YOUR FINANCIAL PYRAMID**	**145**
Chapter 41	Early Childhood: Birth to Age 12	146
Chapter 42	Your Child's Education Fund	148
Chapter 43	Wealth-Producing Teenagers	150
Chapter 44	The Power Learning Years	155
Chapter 45	Family Mode	159
Chapter 46	Essential Financial Protection for Young Families	164
Chapter 47	Your First Home	175
Chapter 48	Should I Buy or Rent	183
Chapter 49	Should I Contribute to My RRSP or Pay Down My Mortgage	184
Chapter 50	The Power Earning Years	187
PART 5	**PRE-RETIREMENT PLANNING**	**197**
Chapter 51	The Challenges of Retirement	198
Chapter 52	Gifts of Charity	200
Chapter 53	Seasons in the Sun	202
Chapter 54	Planning for Death	206
Chapter 55	Self-Actualization	208

Introduction

"The road to success is always under construction."

Anonymous

Why do some people, who have less income than you do, have so much more financial freedom? They seem to be doing what they want, and when they want. They have a calm and happy demeanour. They appear to be satisfied with their life as a whole.

They are people who have it all—enough money to do the things they want and, just as important, the time to enjoy it. That is the ultimate goal of financial independence—to be able to meet present needs and to be prepared to meet those needs again in the future, under different circumstances.

Like it or not, change is the essence of our lives. We spend our first 20 or so years learning to take a productive place in society. It is then up to us to produce for 40 or so more years before "retirement" is upon us. In those 40 years, much money will pass through our hands. Did you know that earning $2500 a month, for 40 years, will result in total earnings of over $1.2 million? That's right. With an annual salary of $30,000, you will have been a millionaire by virtue of your gross earnings. Think of your potential lifetime gross earnings if you make $3,000, $4,000 or even $10,000 each month.

You need to manage these large sums of money you will earn in your lifetime. Money is the tool you will use to acquire wealth—an abundance of assets, affluence and financial freedom.

It is up to you to make sure most of the money you make stays in your hands. That's the tricky part, of course. Never forget that the object of the time and effort you put towards wealth creation is to keep as much "net profit"—that is, income left over after you have paid expenses such as taxes, food, clothing and shelter—as possible. Line your own pockets—not someone else's.

To take control of your financial destiny, you need a plan—a blueprint or road map. This is where a custom-designed money-management plan comes in. It will guide you down the road to financial independence. You can design it yourself, or you can seek professional help for these purposes.

However, to build an effective financial plan you must have a good understanding of the products and services available to you, as well as what motivates you to feel satisfied at different stages of your life. Motivation is the source of all our activities. Whether or not we reach our personal goals is dependent upon our personal level of motivation. What motivated you to buy this book, for example? You obviously felt dissatisfied in some way with the state of your money management affairs. You have a need to make some changes and possess the drive and desire to put them into action.

As you read this book, you will begin a journey down the road to success. Along the way, you will measure and celebrate your achievements and analyze and learn from your setbacks. You will find that with your money management plan at your side, decision-making will be possible and even enjoyable. With every well-researched and focused decision, you will gain the experience you need to take control of your future.

At some points during the journey you will be the passenger; at others you will take the wheel of the car. You will be prepared for flat tires and detours. You'll know what to do if you take a wrong turn. You'll be ready for the unpredictable weather along the way: when there is fog, you'll slowly find your way through, knowing that it will lift eventually. When the hail pummels down on you, you'll practice damage control. And when the sun shines hot and bright, you'll be able to sit back and enjoy the day and not be offput that a thunderstorm could be building on the horizon.

PART 1

TOOLS FOR ESTABLISHING A MONEY MANAGEMENT PLAN

CHAPTER 1
Initiating Change

Motivation—the drive to satisfy your needs and relieve discomfort—is a critical component of creating a money management plan. So is teamwork.

In writing the book, this author is motivated to help you successfully create and implement your own money management plan. Call it "custom-designing"—providing you with the tools you need to make it work for you. The motivating factor? The satisfaction that comes with knowing our efforts have helped you take control of your financial destiny.

You, on the other hand, must realize that you have the power to determine your fate in life. If you are unhappy or overwhelmed by your current state of affairs, you can bring about the changes required to relieve the frustration you feel. Frustration can initiate action. When you feel frustrated, you become aware that you are not achieving the results you expect for the time and energy you are expending. In fact, the more frustrated you feel, the greater will be your desire for change.

In being motivated to take control of your future, you will face a number of barriers to initiating change, both personally and within your family. Here's why.

INERTIA

This is an interesting word. It is defined in *Webster's Dictionary* as both a lack of skill and a disinclination to move or act. Most people find "personal inertia" to be the biggest barrier towards taking control of their destiny. It's simply easier to "keep things as they are . . . for now." Let's "worry about the future later." Or, "we can always learn the skills required for change when change is upon us." We've all had those thoughts.

Change will either be forced upon you or managed by you. Either way, it will take you out of your routine, make you give up your spot on the couch and force you to change your habits. This will seem like such hard work and, at first, it is. Once you realize that change is up to you, you will find yourself searching for information, rearranging your thoughts and seeking time to create, nurture and develop your plans.

To create any type of change within an organization—including a family—you must follow a process.

It is important to ensure that everyone is receptive to the changes you wish to bring about. Introducing change without having your team members "on board" is sure to fail. Allow your team members to "buy in" by obtaining their feedback. You might be surprised at the response. You will also feel assured that your plan will be carried out, even if you can not be there to manage it.

You might find, for example, that there are problems you had not considered or solutions to existing problems you had not identified. But most importantly, a family brainstorming event on a subject as important as your financial independence will eliminate resistance to change. All must be motivated to make the new plan work.

Don't forget to include in your "team" the help of qualified professionals you feel comfortable with. Your tax practitioner, lawyer, insurance broker, real estate agent, stock broker or investment advisor, and banker are all important figures who will assist you in making the right decisions. How well you communicate your objectives to your professional team will greatly advance your progress.

> **MONEY MANAGEMENT TIP 1**
>
> Choose your money management team carefully and make sure your entire family is behind your efforts.

FEAR

Just as motivation to satisfy our needs is the source of all our activities, fear is a great inhibitor of action. Fearful emotions such as worry and anxiety come about when we are not prepared to face an anticipated future event, such as our retirement, the loss of our job or business, or the death of a loved one.

Fear is defined in the *Concise Oxford Dictionary* as the "painful emotion caused by impending danger or evil; a state of alarm or dread of a future event." People feel fear when they don't have control over their destiny. Fear brings about hesitation and apprehension. Fear causes one to shrink away from action and cripples decision-making. Therefore, it inhibits the ability to seize upon opportunities in your lifetime. For the purposes of creating and implementing an effective financial plan, you must conquer your fears and take control. Fortunately, your financial plan will help you do this.

> **MONEY MANAGEMENT TIP 2**
> Conquer your fears of financial decision-making by preparing a money management plan.

AN INABILITY TO MAKE DECISIONS

If you fear decision-making, always remember this: Not making a decision is a decision. Follow these steps to help you conquer your fear of decision-making:

Steps to Making a Decision

1. Write down exactly what decision you need to make.
2. Write down why you want to make this decision.
3. Write down all the actions that are required to implement the decision.
4. Write down all the advantages of making the decision.
5. Write down all the possible downsides of the decision.
6. Write down all the advantages of not making the decision.
7. Write down all the disadvantages of not making the decision.
8. Make your decision.
9. Establish an exact date as to when results of your decision should happen.
10. Read your decision out loud.

Try this new process with this objective: *I must make the decision to implement a money management plan.*

CHAPTER 2
Effective Decision-Making

Well, you're committed now. You've made the decision to custom design and implement a money management plan. That's great! You now have the insight you need to analyze what a decision is. As well, you are on your way to obtaining one of the greatest assets you can possess: *Wisdom*.

Wisdom is the by-product of decision-making. Wisdom is a required element of our money management plan. We must acquire it in order to make important judgment calls about our future. The best way to acquire the wisdom we need to make effective judgments is to start making decisions. When you start making decisions frequently, you'll soon find one of two things will happen:

1. *Your decision will be wrong* and you'll fail in achieving your goal. Accept that this indeed will happen in your life. Failure gives you the experience you need to learn and not make the same mistake again.

2. *Your decision will be right*, in which case you'll achieve your goal and experience satisfaction. In this case, you'll make a note to follow the same process or make the same moves again, whenever the need in question arises again.

Either way, if you are prepared for the outcome of both right and wrong decisions, you always come out a winner because the combination of positive and negative experiences will bless you with wisdom. When you possess both experience and knowledge, you will have the power to apply them to circumstances in your life.

A decision-maker is one who is empowered to control his or her own destiny.

> **MONEY MANAGEMENT TIP 3**
>
> To make a decision an effective one, whether it is right or wrong, learn to manage the outcome.

Managing the Outcome of Decision-making

1. Know what you want.
2. Set your standards for risk and reward.
3. Have a long-term focus.
4. Think through your "Action Plan."

You can accomplish this by creating a Personal Mission Statement, followed up with goals and objectives that can be measured and evaluated.

CHAPTER 3
Your Personal Mission Statement

Most organizations have a mission statement. This is a statement that describes the divine purpose of the organization—the underlying reason for all the activities of the firm and how they are carried out.

A personal mission statement is much the same thing. It embodies what our dreams are made of and provides insight to our future. It requires initial soul-searching and continuous revisiting as you move through various predefined life cycles:

Life Cycles

Dependency:	Birth to Age 12
Wealth-Producing Teenagers:	Ages 13 to 18
Power Learning Years:	Ages 19 to 25
Family Mode:	Ages 20 to 40
Power Earning Years:	Ages 40 to 60
Your Golden Years:	Ages 60 and beyond

Your Personal Mission Statement is probably the most difficult statement you will ever put to paper. It should be no longer than a dozen or so words. It should be simple to remember and provide direction when you veer off the road to success and get lost. The Mission Statement is your compass.

It will embody your expectations and your values, those things you feel are worth working for. Think of it as your Family Motto.

The purpose of your Family Motto? Well, Roy Disney probably said it best with this quote:

"It's not hard to make decisions when you know what your values are."

To create a Personal Mission Statement or Family Motto, do the following exercise together with your family:

1. *Identify your values:* Your values will guide every decision you make. What are the things that are worth the most to you? Choose from the following list, or add your own opinion:

Love	Health	Freedom	Security
Power	Achievement	Happiness	Fun
Standards	Acceptance	Integrity	Confidence

Others:

_____   _____
_____   _____
_____   _____

2. *Compose your Personal Mission Statement:* In one sentence, write down the guiding principals that will act as your compass in developing and maintaining your money management plan. For example:

"The Smith Family's mission is to be financially independent, while respecting health and relationships, and giving back to nature and society whenever possible."

A good start, but not precise enough.

"The Smith Family will care for each other first and, wherever possible, contribute to their community."

Too long. Image your 15-year-old buying into that!

"Integrity and achievement for health and happiness."

The components are there, but does it meet the test of effectiveness? Does it provide direction?

"Plan for prosperity, live with integrity, achieve standards of excellence."

Better.

3. *Now compose the first goal of your Personal Mission Statement:* Remember, don't make it "Mission Impossible." It could be as simple as the following:

"Our goal is to have the resources required to satisfy the needs of the present and future."

You now possess the guiding principles surrounding every personal and financial decision you make. The next step is to build an *Action Plan* around your goal. To do this, you must determine your exact objectives—those things you will aim to do.

MONEY MANAGEMENT TIP 4

Prepare a specific financial goal that will guide you throughout your decision-making process.

CHAPTER 4
Documenting Your Net Worth

In order to set out the objectives of your financial plan, you must first analyze your current financial status. To do so, you need to create a net worth statement. This will require some information gathering.

> **MONEY MANAGEMENT TIP 5**
>
> Prepare a net worth statement at least once every year to chart your financial position as of a specific date.

YOUR PERSONAL NET WORTH STATEMENT
Date Prepared: _____

MY ASSETS

CURRENT ASSETS:
(These are assets that can be quickly converted to cash)   **Term   Yield   Total A**

Cash in Chequing/Savings Accounts:
Account #_____ Bank/Branch_____ _____ ____% $_____
Account #_____ Bank/Branch_____ _____ ____% $_____
Account #_____ Bank/Branch_____ _____ ____% $_____

Investments: i) Non-Registered (held outside an RRSP)
GICs Held:
Certificate #_____ Financial Institution_____ _____ ____% $_____
Certificate #_____ Financial Institution_____ _____ ____% $_____
Certificate #_____ Financial Institution_____ _____ ____% $_____
Certificate #_____ Financial Institution_____ _____ ____% $_____

Canada Savings Bonds Held:
Certificate #_____ Financial Institution_____ _____ ____% $_____
Certificate #_____ Financial Institution_____ _____ ____% $_____
Certificate #_____ Financial Institution_____ _____ ____% $_____

    Subtotal Column A $_____

Balance Forward, Column A $_____

Treasury Bills Held:
Certificate #_____ Acquisition Price $_____ (At Maturity)_____ $_____
Certificate #_____ Acquisition Price $_____ (At Maturity)_____ $_____
Certificate #_____ Acquisition Price $_____ (At Maturity)_____ $_____
Certificate #_____ Acquisition Price $_____ (At Maturity)_____ $_____

Other Government Bonds/Debentures: **Term   Yield**
Certificate #_____ Held By:_____ _____ _____% $_____
Certificate #_____ Held By:_____ _____ _____% $_____
Certificate #_____ Held By:_____ _____ _____% $_____
Certificate #_____ Held By:_____ _____ _____% $_____

Other Debt Instruments:
Mortgages: Debtor:_____ _____% $_____
Mortgage-Backed Securities_____ _____% $_____
Strip Bonds: Acquisition Price $_____ (At Maturity)_____ $_____

Equities (Stocks, Common or Preferred; Mutual Funds)
Name_____ Acquisition Cost_____ Acquired_____ $_____
Name_____ Acquisition Cost_____ Acquired_____ $_____
Name_____ Acquisition Cost_____ Acquired_____ $_____
Name_____ Acquisition Cost_____ Acquired_____ $_____

Investments ii) Registered (held inside an RRSP)

GICs Held   **Term   Yield**
Certificate #_____ Financial Institution_____ _____ _____% $_____
Certificate #_____ Financial Institution_____ _____ _____% $_____
Certificate #_____ Financial Institution_____ _____ _____% $_____
Certificate #_____ Financial Institution_____ _____ _____% $_____

Canada Savings Bonds Held:
Certificate #_____ Financial Institution_____ _____ _____% $_____
Certificate #_____ Financial Institution_____ _____ _____% $_____
Certificate #_____ Financial Institution_____ _____ _____% $_____

Treasury Bills Held:
Certificate #_____ Acquisition Price $_____ (At Maturity)_____ $_____
Certificate #_____ Acquisition Price $_____ (At Maturity)_____ $_____
Certificate #_____ Acquisition Price $_____ (At Maturity)_____ $_____
Certificate #_____ Acquisition Price $_____ (At Maturity)_____ $_____

Other Government Bonds/Debentures: **Term   Yield**
Certificate #_____ Held By:_____ _____ _____% $_____
Certificate #_____ Held By:_____ _____ _____% $_____
Certificate #_____ Held By:_____ _____ _____% $_____
Certificate #_____ Held By:_____ _____ _____% $_____

Subtotal Column A $_____

Balance Forward, Column A		$_____

Other Debt Instruments:
Mortgages: Debtor:_____ _____ ___% $_____
Mortgage-Backed Securities_____ _____ ___% $_____
Strip Bonds: Acquisition Price $_____ (At Maturity)_____ $_____

Equities (Stocks, Common or Preferred; Mutual Funds)
Name_____ Acquisition Cost_____ Acquired_____ $_____
Name_____ Acquisition Cost_____ Acquired_____ $_____
Name_____ Acquisition Cost_____ Acquired_____ $_____
Name_____ Acquisition Cost_____ Acquired_____ $_____

Insurance Policies Held	**Face Amount**	**Cash Values**
Policy Insurer_____	$_____	$_____
Policy Insurer_____	$_____	$_____
Policy Insurer_____	$_____	$_____
Policy Insurer_____	$_____	$_____

Other Current Assets:
_____ $_____
_____ $_____

OTHER ASSETS:

Goodwill in Business Interests $_____

Real Estate:

Personal Residences:		**Cost**	**FMV**
Principal _____	Date Acquired_____	$_____	$_____
Cottage_____	Date Acquired_____	$_____	$_____
Other Vacation_____	Date Acquired_____	$_____	$_____

Revenue Properties:
_____	Date Acquired_____	$_____	$_____
_____	Date Acquired_____	$_____	$_____

Other Personal Use Properties (describe)		**Cost**	**FMV**
Car #1_____	Date Acquired_____	$_____	$_____
Car #2_____	Date Acquired_____	$_____	$_____
Boat_____	Date Acquired_____	$_____	$_____
Furs_____	Date Acquired_____	$_____	$_____
Jewellery_____	Date Acquired_____	$_____	$_____
Collections_____	Date Acquired_____	$_____	$_____
Furniture/Household Effects:		$_____	$_____
Other_____		$_____	$_____

    TOTAL OF ALL ASSETS $_____A

| Total Assets forward | $_____ A |

LIABILITIES AND NET WORTH — Value B

Credit Card Balances:
Card #1 _____ $_____
Card #2 _____ $_____
Card #3 _____ $_____

Current Bills Payable: _____ $_____
_____ $_____
_____ $_____
_____ $_____

Tax Instalment Payments Due $_____

Mortgages on Principal Residence $_____

Mortgages on Other Properties (list)
_____ $_____
_____ $_____
_____ $_____
_____ $_____

Bank Loans (describe)
_____ $_____
_____ $_____
_____ $_____

Margin Accounts (describe)
_____ $_____
_____ $_____

Life Insurance Policy Loans (describe)
_____ $_____
_____ $_____

Other (describe)
_____ $_____
_____ $_____

| **TOTAL OF ALL LIABILITIES** | $_____ | $_____ |

| **FAMILY NET WORTH (A minus B)** | $_____ B |

This is a snapshot of where you stand today, financially. Where would you like to be? Tomorrow? A year from now? Five years from now?

CHAPTER 5
Charting Your Current Cash Flow

During the recession of the early 1990s, many otherwise healthy firms teetered on the edge of bankruptcy. Some made it through; others did not. The reason? The failures ran out of cash. When money flows out faster or sooner than it flows in, you've got serious troubles, particularly if there is no "emergency fund" to fall back on.

In the introductory comments of this book we talked about helping you out of the fog. This is the whole reason behind a cash flow statement.

A cash flow statement is really your personal income and expense statement. It tells you the results of your family financial "operations"—the inflow and outflow of cash on a monthly basis.

You can prepare one statement for combined family earnings and expenditures, or you can have each income producer prepare one.

The object is to find out how much money is coming in every month, before taxes, and how much is flowing back out.

To start the process, prepare a cash flow statement for the current month. Be as complete as possible in listing all items. Our format is only a guide. You can revise it or create one that better matches your financial picture, if you like. Once you are satisfied that you have listed all income and expenses, prepare a cash flow statement for each month of the upcoming year. Anticipate bonuses, raises, as well as new expenses or outlays.

Let's prepare one now for your family, for the past month:

CASH FLOW STATEMENT
Month of _____

INCOME   A   Analysis

Gross Employment Income:
   Spouse 1 $_____
   Spouse 2 $_____
   Subtotal $_____ $_____   _____

Self-Employment Net Income $_____   _____

Government Assistance:
   CTB[1] $_____
   CPP[2] Benefits $_____
   OAS[3] $_____
   UIC[4] Benefits $_____
   Social Assistance $_____
   Workers' Compensation $_____
   Federal Supplements $_____
   Provincial Supplements $_____
   Other $_____
   Subtotal $_____ $_____   _____

From Private Pensions:
   RRIFs $_____
   RRSPs $_____
   Annuities $_____
   Superannuation $_____
   Foreign Pensions $_____
   Other $_____
   Subtotal $_____ $_____   _____

From Investments:
   Interest $_____
   Dividends $_____
   Rental Income $_____
   Other $_____
   Subtotal $_____ $_____   _____

From Sale of Capital Assets (attach list) $_____   _____
From Alimony or Maintenance $_____   _____

From Other Sources:
   Scholarships $_____
   Debt Held by You[5] $_____
   Other: _____: $_____
   Subtotal $_____ $_____   _____

Total Income $_____ A

[1]Child Tax Benefit   [2]Canada Pension Plan   [3]Old Age Security   [4]Unemployment Insurance
[5]Mortgages, notes, etc. owed to you by others

Total Income from prior page		$_____ A

OUTLAYS	**B**	**Analysis**
Source Deductions:		
Income Taxes	$_____	
CPP/UIC	$_____	
Subtotal	$_____	$_____ _____
Groceries		$_____ _____
Clothing		$_____ _____
Footware		$_____ _____
Entertainment		$_____ _____
Utilities:		
Telephone	$_____	
Heat	$_____	
Electricity	$_____	
Water	$_____	
Subtotal	$_____	$_____ _____
Repairs and Maintenance		$_____ _____
Mortgage Payments	$_____	$_____ _____
Insurance Payments	$_____	$_____ _____
Car Payments	$_____	$_____ _____
Savings		
RRSPs	$_____	
Canada Savings Bonds	$_____	
Vacation Fund	$_____	
Education Fund	$_____	
Other	$_____	
Subtotal	$_____	$_____ _____
Other:		
Tax Instalment Payments	$_____	
Other Loan Payments:	$_____	
Gifts	$_____	
Pharmacy	$_____	
Miscellaneous	$_____	
Subtotal	$_____	$_____ _____
Total Outlays		$_____ B
Net Cash Flow (A minus B)		$_____

Now complete a 12-month record sheet to show your monthly surplus or deficit and your cumulative cash flow at the end of each month. A thirteenth column will summarize your totals for each line item.

> **MONEY MANAGEMENT TIP 6**
> Prepare an annual cash flow statement to establish positive and negative monthly cash flows.

You should take note that one subgroup of our outlays is "savings." Budget to pay some of your income into savings and vacation funds. If you don't, no one else will.

CHAPTER 6 Establishing Direction

The next step is to take a hard look at your family's net worth and cash flow. How do you feel about it? What is reflected on your personal balance sheet is a snapshot of the results of your past efforts. Are you proud of your accomplishments? Good for you! You deserve a pat on the back.

Are you appalled? Don't be dismayed. Now is the time to turn your affairs around.

To do so, you must set very explicit objectives. This exercise is difficult because you will be forced to think through exactly what results you expect for the time and effort you expend.

Before you can take aim, you must establish direction.

HOW TO ESTABLISH DIRECTION

1. *Begin by brainstorming*. Document all of the actions needed to improve your family's net worth and cash flow statement. Ask each family member for their input. For example:

   I wish to make $300 a month more.
   I wish to pay off my credit cards.
   I wish to acquire a cottage.
   I wish to pay less tax.

2. *Put a time limit on each wish.* For example:
   I wish to make $300 a month more—within four months.
   I wish to pay off my credit cards—within six months.
   I wish to acquire a cottage—one year from now.
   I wish to pay less tax—immediately.
3. *List ways you can make each wish a reality.* How can you do more with the same—or fewer—resources?
   a. Shop around for the best price:
      - get three quotes for every new product or service you acquire
      - use coupons and watch for "dollar coupon days"
      - consider buying used vs. new
      - ask competitors to match prices—even at major department stores
      - read flyers and then shop by phone to get the best prices
      - be focused: know what you want before you get into a store and leave with what you intended to buy
   b. Learn how to negotiate for the best price. Be firm; it's your money.
   c. Acquire the knowledge to make the best decision.
   d. Create new money: get a part-time job to pay for the wish. Increase the return on your current investments. Think of ways to cut down on a current expenses and save the money for the possessions you want:
      - sell one or some of your possessions
      - pay down your mortgage faster and invest the savings
      - stop buying with credit cards and paying outrageous interest
      - lower the amount of money you spend on gifts
      - eat more pasta and less red meat
      - sew your own clothes
      - wrap gifts in newspaper and top with red ribbon
      - cut down by half the amount of toothpaste and shampoo you use each day
      - store rain water in a barrel
      - get a library card and then take your family there for videos as well as books and magazines
      - winter-proof your house with double- or triple-pane windows and weather-stripping
      - check the fireplace: is it energy efficient?
        - close vents and damper when not in use
      - let the sun in to warm your home
      - save on utility costs wherever possible:
        - review all bills and estimates

- challenge estimates immediately
- shower with a friend(!)
- handwash dishes (cuts down on soap costs, too)
- fix leaky faucets, hoses, toilets, etc.
- turn down temperature on hot water tank (convert to gas if you have electric)
- put timers on lights and turn them off when not in use
- increase use of microwave to save electricity costs
- sign up for utility-volume purchase plans, especially for telephone and gas
- review the need for 100-watt bulbs when 60-watt bulbs will do
- review your telephone expenses—would a fax machine or modem be cheaper in the long run?
- call after hours to save long-distance charges
- use a calling card
- clean your own house, cut your own grass and shovel your own snow
- buy cereal without sugar coating
- start a vegetable garden
- go to garage sales
- ride public transit and buy tickets instead of paying cash.

e. Ask yourself, "Can I live without this?"
- cable TV
- a second car
- eating out at lunchtime
- new clothes
- out-of-country vacations
- the extra telephone/cellular phone
- brand-name vs. generic products
- new vs. used furniture and appliances
- new vs. used car
- personalized envelopes
- magazine subscriptions
- store-bought baked goods
- Friday-night pizzas
- air conditioning.

f. Review your prior tax returns to see if you missed anything that would reap an additional refund. While prior filed returns are listed last in this section, they are often the most lucrative source of large amounts of new money. In Canada, since 1985 we have faced the most complicated and far-reaching tax and pension reform in our history. Chances are that you may have missed a tax provision that is worth thousands of dollars to you—particularly if you missed it and have been entitled to it every year since 1985. You can request adjustments to your return that far back, so dig them out and review them soon.

4. *Chart the risks your family faces in the future.* These are uncontrollable events you must plan for. Choose from the list below and include others you may think of:

Premature Death	Job Loss	Disability
Medical Expenses	Loss of Property	Loss of Business
Tax Hikes	Political Unrest	Property Breakdown
Re-education	Inflation Rates	Interest Rates
Separation	Divorce	Relocation
Early Retirement	Unplanned Births	

Others: _____ _____ _____

_____ _____ _____

5. *List ways in which you can protect yourself against the risks of the unknown.*
   - Premature Death: life insurance, a will, an estate plan, *savings*.
   - Job Loss: *savings*, wage loss plans, second income, home-based business, health maintenance.
   - Disability: insurance, *savings*, CPP Disability Fund, Social Assistance, wage loss plans, health plans.
   - Medical Costs: health insurance plans, *savings*, provincial health plans.
   - Property Loss: liability insurance, *savings*.
   - Loss of Business: creditor-proofing, *savings*, credit rating, networking.
   - Tax Hikes: RRSPs, investment diversification, knowledge, income splitting, make more money, review tax saving options.
   - Political Unrest: *savings*, second residences.
   - Property Breakdown: property insurance, *savings*.
   - Re-education: *savings*, student loan applications, UIC benefits.
   - Inflation: investment diversification, asset mix.
   - Interest Rates: investment diversification, asset mix.
   - Separation: *savings*, prenuptial agreement, spousal agreement.
   - Divorce: *savings*, prenuptial agreement, spousal agreement.
   - Relocation: *savings*, good real estate investments.
   - Early Retirement: RRSPs, CPP retirement fund, superannuation, *savings*, deferred profit-sharing plans, annuities, cash values from life insurance policies, investments.

Well, if your list resembles ours in any way, you'll find it doesn't take a rocket scientist to deduce the following obvious facts:

> **MONEY MANAGEMENT TIPS 7, 8 & 9**
>
> Savings are the primary way to protect yourself from the unexpected.
>
> Investment diversification strategies will protect you from the economic roller-coaster of inflation, deflation, interest rate fluctuation, market fluctuations and increasing taxes.
>
> The right kind of insurance will protect you when things go wrong.

By documenting your current net worth and cash flow, and identifying the potential financial risks you and your family face, you can plan to rearrange your priorities so that you can save, diversify and protect yourself. We have, therefore, arrived at the *primary long-term objectives* of your financial plan:

1. To save money.
2. To diversify investments.
3. To protect your family from major setbacks beyond your control.

You might be asking yourself: "How do we start saving money, if we have difficulty making ends meet now?" This is where our *short-term objectives* come in. Write down your specific action plan for meeting your primary objectives. It might look similar to that of our fictional Smith family:

Short-Term Objectives or "Action Plan" of the Smith Family

1. To save $1,000 in an RRSP this year.
2. To save the Child Tax Benefit in a separate "Education Account" set up for the children.
3. To increase our mortgage payments by 10 per cent.
4. To increase and diversify our insurance policies.
5. To have the stay-at-home spouse get a part-time job.
6. To invest in a Canada Savings Bond through the payroll plan at work.
7. To pay off our credit cards.
8. To track our results.

Start an action plan now. Rearrange priorities to create new disposable dollars with existing resources.

CHAPTER 7
Implementing Objectives and Tracking Results

You are now ready to implement your personal and financial goals and objectives. As previously discussed, this means you must enable change in your life. To get started quickly and easily, you need:

1. A specific, organized workplace.
2. A formula for results.

CREATING A WORKPLACE

If you acquired a new vehicle today, you would likely store it in your garage (if there's room!). If you liked refinishing furniture, you would find a special spot in your home devoted solely to this activity. Likewise, your financial plan must develop in a separate workplace, consisting of the following basic supplies:

1. *Your desktop:* A quiet place in a home office or bedroom, or even the dining-room table is acceptable, provided you can spread out your documents and work on an uninterrupted basis, and then store them in a safe and orderly place for easy access the next time.

2. *Your files:* This might be a series of documents in a computer program, or a ledger book or sheets acquired from your local office supplies store. At the very least, it should be a package of lined loose-leaf paper that is three-hole punched. It's a good idea to invest in a three-hole punch if you don't already have one.

3. *Your filing cabinet:* This could be a special drawer or an actual filing cabinet set aside solely for your money management documentation.

4. *Four three-ring binders* with pockets on the inside front and back sleeves. Label the first one "Income," the second "Expenses," the third "Statements," and the fourth, "Operations Manual." This operations manual will help you record the strategies that worked for you—and those that didn't. Like a diary, it will allow you to set up notes and reminders about your financial affairs.

5. *Envelopes:* Acquire a package of 24, 9-inch x 12-inch envelopes, open at the top, not the side. Label each set of 12 at the top righthand side with a month of the year. Each will be used to store "hard copy" documentation to verify deposits, cheques and other income. Put six of those envelopes in the front pocket of your "Income" binder, and the other six in the back. Do the same for your second set of envelopes—those that will hold your receipts for expenses—in the front and back pockets of your "Expenses" binder.

6. *Calculator:* If you don't already have one, buy a good calculator—one with a tape. If you have a personal computer, learn to use a spreadsheet program.

To save time in acquiring your basic money management kit, create a shopping list; then save time and money by calling for three quotes, for example:

Shopping List for Office Supplies

Description of Item:	Budget	Quote 1	Quote 2	Quote 3
Filing cabinet (used)	$100.00	_____	_____	_____
Ruled ledger sheets or a package of loose leaf	3.00	_____	_____	_____
A 3-hole punch	15.00	_____	_____	_____
24 open top 9-in. x 12-in. envelopes @ approximately 10 cents each	2.40	_____	_____	_____
4 3-ring binders (2-in. rings) @ approximately $5.00 each	20.00	_____	_____	_____
A financial calculator	40.00	_____	_____	_____
Pens, pencils, eraser	5.00	_____	_____	_____
Approximate Outlay:	$185.40	_____	_____	_____

A FORMULA FOR RESULTS

In creating our workplace, we have taken two very critical steps. We have made the decision to design a financial plan and we have installed the first action-oriented approach to implement it. In this very basic exercise we have already started the maintenance of our plan by introducing two new family policies: the creation of a written report—our shopping list—and the requirement to call retailers for three quotes on our proposed purchases. The result will be the acquisition, at the best possible price, of the office supplies we need to develop and maintain our money management plan.

To put this procedure into an arithmetical formula, consider the following:

> **MONEY MANAGEMENT TIP 10**
>
> Results = Planning + Procedures + Action + Analysis

Our shopping procedure embodied several key guiding principals you must always keep in mind in gaining control over your money:

> **MONEY MANAGEMENT TIPS 11, 12, 13 & 14**
>
> Your money is always either in your pocket, or someone else's. Better in yours.
>
> When shopping for products, services or professional advisors, always get three quotes. By calling for the best price, quality, knowledge and service, you will save time and money.
>
> Keep source documents, such as purchase orders, invoices and contracts, for tracking your money. File copies readily at hand for tax purposes and creation of your cash flow, net worth statements and will.
>
> Write down your policies and procedures as they develop. Chart both successful and unsuccessful actions. This written record of your actions will become your "money management roadmap."

CHAPTER 8 Analyzing Results

We now have an idea where our money comes from and where it goes every month, and we know our areas of need. Together with our primary and short-term objectives and a quiet, well-equipped workstation, we can begin to do some analysis to help us get organized.

First, we should become acquainted with methods of evaluation. You can probably find several ways to create new money on close examination, or an "evaluation," of your cash outflow statement. When you evaluate something, you usually apply a type of measurement device.

If you were in school, your performance would be judged by a percentile grade. Sports teams keep scores. To measure financial results, you also need measurement devices. These can include:

1. *Measurement by comparison:* Compare this month to last month; this month this year to this month last year, this year to last year, and so on. You'll soon find that you're doing better, worse or the same as the period you are comparing to. This gives you valuable information for decision-making.

   For example:

	This Year	Last Year	Difference
Total Gross Income:	$50,000	$45,000	+$5,000
Total Expenses:	$46,000	$42,000	+$4,000
Net profit on Disposable Income:	$ 4,000	$ 3,000	+$1,000

   In this case, even though you got a $5,000 raise, you managed to create only $1,000 in new disposable income. Why?

2. *Measurement using percentages:* By analyzing figures on your statements on a common base—that is, so much out of 100—you'll be able to make comparisons more quickly.

   For example, all the money you earn in the month is 100 per cent. Any expenditure line items are a percentage of this number. That is, take each expense and divide it by the total income.

Monthly Income from all sources:	$5,000	100%
Expenses:		
Income Taxes	$1,500	30.0%
House payments	1,285	25.7%
Utilities	300	6.0%
Food	500	10.0%
Clothing	300	6.0%
Other	115	2.3%
Total Expenses:	$4,000	80.0%
Disposable Income:	$1,000	20.0%

   Get the idea? Now go back to Chapter 5 and chart percentiles for your cash flow statement next to column A. How do you compare to the National Average on costing out taxes paid, food, clothing and shelter?

   A table published by the Fraser Institute of Canada in their book *Tax Facts 8* lists figures from their *Canadian Tax Simulator* and Statistics

Canada's *1990 Expenditure Survey*. It shows that in 1992, the average Canadian family, with a total annual income before tax of $74,723, paid the following:

Average Taxes (including indirect taxes)	$23,537	31.5%
Average Shelter Costs	8,903	11.0%
Average Food Costs	7,161	9.6%
Average Clothing Costs	2,986	4.0%

How do your percentages compare? Are you spending more or less than the national average? From these comparisons you can quickly see whether you live in a home that's too expensive for your income, or whether you spend too much on clothing. These comparisons will help you set new objectives and make new decisions.

By the way, there are two other interesting facts in the Fraser Institute document. In 1972, when our federal finances were close to break-even level (that's right, no deficit), and we tackled the first year of a major tax reform, the average Canadian annual income was $14,154 before taxes. In that year we paid:

Average Taxes (including indirect taxes)	$4,203
Average Shelter Costs	1,778
Average Food Costs	1,791
Average Clothing Costs	739

Without the percentages, the numbers mean little to us. Add the percentages and see what happens:

Average Taxes (including indirect taxes)	$4,203	29.7%
Average Shelter Costs	1,778	12.6%
Average Food Costs	1,791	12.7%
Average Clothing Costs	739	5.2%

Now we can compare! There's more to this topic. In the July 1994 issue of *The Fraser Forum*, based on federal and provincial government budgets and estimates, StatsCan data and the Conference Board of Canada's "Research on Provincial Outlooks," it appears that both income and taxes have gone up in Canada:

	1994	1992	Difference
Average Family Income before Tax	$82,108	$74,723	+$7,385(10%)
Total All Taxes	$27,435	$23,537	+$3,898(17%)

Our measurement tools—dollar comparisons and percentiles—give us a good frame of reference for analysis and data, as well as our resulting conclusions.

3. *Measurement using ratios:* A ratio is a quantitative relationship between two numbers determined by the number of times one contains the other, integrally or fractionally.* A ratio can help you make a judgment. Ratios will help you analyze your financial statements or those of companies you may wish to invest in.

Financial statements will generally include a balance sheet, which is a snapshot of the financial position of a particular enterprise, as at a specific date. The basic accounting equation used to produce a balance sheet is

ASSETS =	LIABILITIES +	OWNER'S EQUITY
What the enterprise owns	What the enterprise owes	Net worth or owner's interest in the enterprise *or* excess of assets over liabilities.

Assets can be classified into two groups: a) current assets—those that can be easily converted to cash in the short term, and b) fixed assets—those that can have a useful life of more than one year and are probably depreciable. Example:

CURRENT ASSETS	FIXED ASSETS
cash	equipment
short-term notes	building
accounts receivable	land
marketable securities	vehicles

Liabilities can also be grouped into two categories: a) short term—those that can be paid off within a period of less than one year, and b) long term—those with repayment terms of more than a year. Example:

CURRENT OR SHORT-TERM LIABILITIES	LONG-TERM LIABILITIES
credit cards	payments due periodically
accounts payable	due to long-term debt such as
debts that must be paid within a year	mortgages, loans, promissory notes

You can compare liabilities to equity, assets to liabilities, and so on using ratios. Some common ratios used in analysis include *Quick Ratio* which will help you judge liquidity—how quickly an asset can be turned into cash:

$$\frac{\text{Current Assets**}}{\text{Current Liabilities}} \quad \frac{64{,}000}{34{,}000} = 1.88 \text{ or } 1.88 \text{ to } 1$$

For every $1.00 in current liabilities we have $1.88 in assets that can quickly be converted to cash.

---

* *Concise Oxford Dictionary*
** Cash, Marketable Securities, Accounts Receivable

Alternately, a lender may compare your assets to your liabilities to make a judgment on your ability to pay back a loan. Your current assets ($100,000) divided by current debt ($20,000) computes out to a ratio of 5:1. The closer you are to a ratio of 1:1 (assets and debt are equal), the better loan risk you are. If the ratio is over 1:1, you may be a very good loan risk at the present time.

The best reason to look to ratios in your analysis of your own financial statements, or those of firms you wish to invest in, is that they sum up the control you have over the management of your affairs, as of a specific date and time.

4. *Charting observations:* Armed with some tools for analysis, you can jot down some observations about your net worth or daily financial operations:
   - My taxes are too high: how much would an RRSP investment save me?
   - We spend a lot of money on entertainment. How much can we save if we cut down by 10 per cent?
   - The interest costs on our loans are too high. Perhaps we can refinance at a lower rate to save.
   - My car loan costs 9 per cent annually. Let's pay that off and invest the savings.
   - How much can we cut down our food bills and still eat well?
   - If we cut all of our expenditures by 10 per cent, what dollar amount would we save?
   - If we invest our earnings, how much will our net worth grow?

   As you can see, your systematic analysis will help you find new money for wealth creation.

> **MONEY MANAGEMENT TIP 15**
>
> Learn to measure the results of your actions using comparison percentiles and ratio analysis.

CHAPTER 9
Budgeting for Success

Have you ever heard the saying, "If you're so smart, how come you're not rich?"

Hits home, doesn't it? Most Canadians consider themselves to be well-educated and, well, smart. Most of us have the educational requirements to do our own tax returns and follow a budget. In fact, any readers who are employed in management probably live and die by the budget their company sets out for them.

Despite this, many households have trouble sticking to a budget. A budget's failure will usually be the consequence of two errors:

1. You have set unrealistic goals, and
2. You have set guidelines that are too rigid.

To avoid financial temptations that take you away from the path you have set for yourself, follow these suggestions:

1. *Relax*. It's okay to treat yourself, even when you're on a budget, so build in some fun.
2. *Reach Out*. It's easier to stick to a budget when the whole family is behind you.
3. *Be Keen*. Remember the whole point of a budget is to give you the things you want.
4. *Don't Cheat*. If you are tempted to "fall off the budgeting wagon," think only of the fact that you are robbing yourself of the lovely future you have envisioned.

> **MONEY MANAGEMENT TIP 16**
>
> Always implement your goals and objectives with a budget: the projected income and expenditures over the specific period in which your goals are directed.

Before we delve into the technicalities of budget creation, consider the following ten guiding principles to creating an environment for change:

The Ten Steps of Budgeting Anonymous
1. We admit that our financial affairs need better management.
2. We believe that we have the power to take control of our financial destiny.
3. We have made the commitment to follow a budget.
4. We have listed our short-term goals.
5. We have listed our long-term goals.
6. We have made intelligent assumptions about our future needs.
7. We have listed our current net worth.
8. We understand our cash flow patterns.
9. We want to reach our goals.
10. We are ready to do it!

CHAPTER 10
A Format for Budgeting

A budget is a projection. It is based on our current income and outflow levels and your well-researched assumptions. It projects forward the numbers we would like to achieve to increase our disposable income, and it gives us a way to analyze our efforts.

What is disposable income? It is what is left after all of your obligations for the necessities of life have been met. In our cash flow worksheet, we charted all incoming monies and all outgoing commitments, including savings. Many of you may not have had anything to show or enter on those savings lines. That is likely because there was nothing left for savings after paying for the daily operations of your family.

This should make you mad. It means that everyone else has benefited from your toil and trouble. You have missed the whole point of working. If this has happened to you recently, remember this tip:

> ## MONEY MANAGEMENT TIP 17
> Plan to pay yourself something every month. Budget for savings as you would a basic necessity.

Unless you write savings directly into your budget, you likely won't have any. It doesn't have to be much—just be sure you write it in. Start with a reasonable goal, say, $1,000 a year. That's approximately $2.75 a day, or $19.00 a week, or $83.00 a month.

How much money will you have if you save $2.75 (ignoring interest), every day, until you retire?

Age Today	Years to Age 65	Capital Saved
25	40	$40,150
35	30	$30,113
45	20	$20,075

Now, if you were only successful once in saving $1,000 and you invested that one lump sum in a compounding* 5 per cent investment vehicle, your money would grow as follows:

Years Invested	Value
20	$2,653
30	$4,322
40	$7,040

* Compounding interest is paid on the automatic reinvestment of interest earned plus principal.

> ## MONEY MANAGEMENT TIP 18
> Think of every dollar of disposable income you have as an employee whose job it is to make more money for you.

Now, let's prepare a simple budget for next month, based on your current cash flow statement and your goals and objectives.

Seven Steps to Creating a Budget

1. Prepare a spreadsheet with 13 primary columns—one for every month of the year and a Grand Total Column.
2. Under each primary heading, create four secondary headings:
   Budget   %   Actual   %
3. Gather together all of your source documents:
   • your net worth statement
   • your cash flow statement

4. Find specific source documents required to budget accurately:
   - your pay stubs
   - your investment earning stubs
   - your pension benefit stubs
   - your mortgage statements
   - your bank statements
   - your property tax statement
   - your savings account passports
   - your receipts for consumer goods
   - your car loan payments and receipts for expenses
   - your insurance statements
5. Dig out your income tax return and your income tax instalment payment record to plan for your tax bill, if any.
6. List your income projections. Total income will equal 1 or 100 per cent. Make assumptions about any salary increases, employment perks, self-employment income or investment returns you may be expecting.
7. List your projected expenditures, citing assumptions made (and attaching supporting worksheets if necessary). Compute their value over income to find out what percentage of your income goes to each expenditure type.
8. Total cash outlays and subtract these from total income to arrive at net disposable income (or net loss).
9. Make decisions about the results of your first draft.
10. Refine and finalize your budget.

Now that you have made your plans, take action... follow your "road map" to your financial goal this month by tracking income and espenses carefully. You may be surprised about the degree of control you'll have over your money. Why? Because you will be making decisions based on planning, study and careful thought.

A BUDGET FOR THE MONTH OF _____

Line Item	This Month	%	Last Month	%	Change + or -
A. PROJECTED INCOME:					
Gross Employment Income:					
Spouse 1	$_____	___	$_____	___	_____
Spouse 2	$_____	___	$_____	___	_____
Self-Employment Income	$_____	___	$_____	___	_____
Government Assistance:					
CTB	$_____	___	$_____	___	_____
CPP Benefits	$_____	___	$_____	___	_____
OAS	$_____	___	$_____	___	_____
UIC Benefits	$_____	___	$_____	___	_____
Social Assistance	$_____	___	$_____	___	_____
Worker's Compensation	$_____	___	$_____	___	_____
Federal Supplements	$_____	___	$_____	___	_____
Provincial Supplements	$_____	___	$_____	___	_____
From Private Pensions:					
RRIFs	$_____	___	$_____	___	_____
RRSPs	$_____	___	$_____	___	_____
Annuities	$_____	___	$_____	___	_____
Superannuation	$_____	___	$_____	___	_____
Foreign Pensions	$_____	___	$_____	___	_____
Other	$_____	___	$_____	___	_____
From Investments:					
Interest	$_____	___	$_____	___	_____
Dividends	$_____	___	$_____	___	_____
Rental Income	$_____	___	$_____	___	_____
From Sale/Capital Assets	$_____	___	$_____	___	_____
From Alimony or Maintenance	$_____	___	$_____	___	_____
From Other Sources:					
Scholarships	$_____	___	$_____	___	_____
Debt Held by You	$_____	___	$_____	___	_____
Other:	$_____	___	$_____	___	_____
Total Projected Income	$_____				

DOCUMENTATION OF ASSUMPTIONS

_____
_____
_____
_____
_____
_____

A BUDGET FOR THE MONTH OF _____

Line Item	This Month	%	Last Month	%	Change + or -
A. Projected Income*	$_____	___	$_____	___	___
B. PROJECTED EXPENDITURES:					
Savings:					
RRSPs	$_____	___	$_____	___	___
Canada Savings Bonds	$_____	___	$_____	___	___
Vacation Fund	$_____	___	$_____	___	___
Education Fund	$_____	___	$_____	___	___
Other	$_____	___	$_____	___	___
Source Deductions:					
Income Taxes	$_____	___	$_____	___	___
CPP/UIC	$_____	___	$_____	___	___
Groceries	$_____	___	$_____	___	___
Clothing	$_____	___	$_____	___	___
Footware	$_____	___	$_____	___	___
Entertainment	$_____	___	$_____	___	___
Utilities:					
Telephone	$_____	___	$_____	___	___
Heat	$_____	___	$_____	___	___
Electricity	$_____	___	$_____	___	___
Water	$_____	___	$_____	___	___
Repairs/Maintenance	$_____	___	$_____	___	___
Mortgage Payments	$_____	___	$_____	___	___
Insurance Payments	$_____	___	$_____	___	___
Car Payments					
#1_____	$_____	___	$_____	___	___
#2_____	$_____	___	$_____	___	___
Tax Instalment Payments	$_____	___	$_____	___	___
Credit Cards					
#1_____	$_____	___	$_____	___	___
#2_____	$_____	___	$_____	___	___
Gifts	$_____	___	$_____	___	___
Pharmacy	$_____	___	$_____	___	___
Miscellaneous	$_____	___	$_____	___	___
B. Total Expenditures	$_____	___	$_____	___	___
C. Disposable Income (A–B)	$_____	___	$_____	___	___

* From previous page.

Now prepare a 12-month record sheet to chart your budget for the entire year.

CHAPTER 11
Reconciling the Bank

When your bank statement arrives, do the following simple calculation:

A SIMPLE BANK RECONCILIATION

Date_____

Bank Statement Balance $_____   Chequebook Balance $_____ $_____

Subtract:
Cheques written but
not yet cleared:

_____
_____
_____
_____
_____
_____
_____ ($_____)

Subtract:
Bank Service Charges $_____
Loan Interest
Loan #1_____ $_____
Loan #2_____ $_____
Subtract: Withdrawals
Not Recorded $_____
                    $_____
                    $_____
                    $_____   ($_____)

Add:
Deposits not recorded:

_____
_____
_____ $_____

Subtract:
Pre-Authorized Pmts:

_____ $_____
_____ $_____
_____ $_____
_____ $_____   ($_____)

Other (State + or -)
_____ $_____
_____ $_____
_____ $_____
_____ $_____
_____ $_____
_____ $_____

Add:
Direct Deposits:
_____ $_____
_____ $_____ $_____

Other (State + or -)
_____ $_____
_____ $_____ $_____

REVISED BANK BAL. $_____   REVISED CHBK. BALANCE $_____

DISCREPANCIES:_____
_____
_____

Probably one of the most mundane, yet most necessary aspects of tracking your money, is faithfully to reconcile your bank account each month. That is, compare your monthly bank statement to the balance of funds you are showing in your chequebook. This is especially important in these days of instant tellers, payments by bank cards, and automatic or electronic deposit of funds.

If there are any discrepancies, you could find yourself overdrawn and scrabbling for funds! Make sure this never happens to you. It's expensive, and embarrassing.

> **MONEY MANAGEMENT TIP 19**
>
> Prepare a reconciliation of your bank accounts faithfully every month to keep track of disposable dollars.

CHAPTER 12 Fine-Tuning Your Results

Now that you have prepared your 12-month budget, review your results critically, looking for answers to these three specific questions:

1. Have I created all the new money I need from my existing income sources?
2. Do I have enough insurance coverage to manage the unexpected?
3. How can I increase and diversify my investments to enrich my life now and in retirement?

HAVE I CREATED ALL THE NEW MONEY I NEED FROM MY EXISTING INCOME SOURCES?

You have budgeted savings for yourself, because you have decided to reap more of the fruits of your labour. This is exciting. You must now decide how

to invest and use your savings. Consider the following as primary savings fund categories:
- Your Lifestyle Savings Funds
- The Millionaires' Club Fund

You can start these two savings funds in one of two places: a financial institution such as a bank or at a stock brokerage firm or other investment firm, depending on how much you have.

Lifestyle Savings Funds

These are "must-haves." Generally, these funds accumulate in smaller amounts, and so you have to settle for lower returns until you have a value of $500 or $1,000 accumulated. At that point, you can consider moving the money into a Guaranteed Investment Certificate (GIC), a bond or other fixed-income savings vehicle. Some mutual funds also allow for smaller principal sums. (See Part 2). Consider opening the following accounts:

1. *An emergency fund:* This should represent two to four months of your monthly income that is readily accessible when needed.

2. *Your RRSP:* Critical because this saves you money in two ways:
    a. annually upon filing a tax return by decreasing the tax you pay;
    b. continuous tax-free compounding inside the plan; that is, earnings from interest, dividends or capital gains accumulate tax free within the RRSP until the funds are withdrawn.

    Your RRSP contribution will also create new money that can help you pay for the expenses. For example, assume you are in a 50 per cent tax bracket. Your annual property tax bill is $4,000. You have decided to save $800 a month in an RRSP. At the end of the year, you'll have $9,600 in your RRSP, which is tax deductible, assuming you have that much "RRSP room" available (see Chapter 37). Your tax deduction reaps savings of 50 per cent of your RRSP contribution— or $4,800. You have now created the new money you need to meet your property tax liability—and more.

3. *Education Fund:* Look at your tax return for this need. If your family net income is around $30,000, it is possible that you receive a Child Tax Benefit (CTB) on a monthly basis. If you do, put that money into an account in the name of your child. The account's purpose is simply to

accumulate earnings—interest, for example—on a tax-free basis. As long as you do not "taint" this account with other monies, such as gifts, the interest is taxed in the child's hands. If you continue to qualify for the CTB over the years, this account will grow quickly into your education fund.

And guess what? This return of your hard-earned tax dollars finances your child's education. Make sure you save it faithfully. See Part 3 for ways to increase your Child Tax Benefit through proper tax planning.

4. *Vacation Fund:* Pack any money you save through cost-cutting or shrewd investing directly into this fund. Create it by buying Canada Savings Bonds through a payroll plan. Some call it the "don't see it, can't spend it" plan. Don't forget to write off the carrying charge on your tax return. This is where you get to treat yourself. Wise money managers can afford to take vacations.

> **MONEY MANAGEMENT TIP 20**
>
> Create three lifestyle savings funds: Emergency, RRSP and Education. Then budget for a vacation fund.

The Millionaires' Club Fund

Go ahead—boldly write the name of your account across your passbook cover. This is the account that's going to house the capital that will give you the financial independence you have always dreamed of. It will be made up of numerous sources, including:

1. *New money:* This is additional money you make outside of your regular earnings, such as:
   - a bonus
   - money from a part-time job
   - earnings from a part-time business
   - money from the sale of a personal asset
   - the interest savings from your paid-off credit cards
   - your tax refund or Child Tax Benefit/GST Credits.

2. *Gifts:* Any time you come into money, from a parent or relative, playing the lottery or receipt of an inheritance or insurance policy, put the money in your Millionaires' Club Fund.

Remember your goals: financial independence in retirement. To have a comfortable monthly income flow, you must start saving now.

> **MONEY MANAGEMENT TIP 21**
>
> Plan to create new disposable dollars by increasing your productivity and that of your money.

DO I HAVE ENOUGH INSURANCE COVERAGE TO MANAGE THE UNEXPECTED?

Is your family protected if something happens to the main breadwinners? What standard of living must be maintained at a minimum if you are hit by a bus, or your spouse is crippled? If you do not have life or disability insurance, plan to make an appointment with representatives of at least three firms to discuss your coverage and cost options.

When you speak to an insurance salesperson about life and disability insurance, be very candid about the investment you may wish to make. Insurance coverage can be both long term and short term, with many different options and costs. Make a mental note to buy the best insurance policy for your needs.

For example, you may find in your research of insurance plans that most disability insurance plans will cover only a portion of your current income. It will still be up to you and your investments to cover the rest.

Or you may find that your need for higher levels of life insurance are now—when your children are still dependent upon you. You may, therefore, wish to pay for more or different coverage now and deal with your long-term wealth creation through other savings vehicles—such as securities or other assets. If you are clear about your needs, your insurance salesperson can do the best job for you.

In short, the primary purpose of any insurance policy you buy is to protect your dependants from financial disaster. So make the very best use of every after-tax dollar that it will take to make sure you have enough insurance. Do not buy too much or the wrong kind of insurance. How much is enough? If you have already acquired enough assets to allow your family to live in the standard of living you wish for them in case of your premature death, you probably need only enough insurance to cover the cash flow requirements generated by the tax and other specific consequences of death.

Shop for three insurance companies to help you find the best insurance policy mix for you, and prepare to interview each one. See Chapter 46 for interview tips.

HOW CAN I INCREASE AND DIVERSIFY MY INVESTMENTS TO ENRICH MY LIFE NOW AND IN RETIREMENT?

To answer this question, you need a good understanding of the relationship between time and money.

To find out more, read on to Part 2: "Options for Putting Your Money to Work."

OPTIONS FOR PUTTING YOUR MONEY TO WORK

CHAPTER 13
Putting Your Dollars to Work

You're probably convinced by now that you have to save money to get ahead. But what if you just don't have anything to spare?

> **MONEY MANAGEMENT TIP 22**
>
> Start with a dollar a day. Just one loonie. Everyone—even you—can save that much. Then apply the theory of maximized yield, minimized risk, and compounding frequency to start your family nest egg.

What's a dollar a day? Would you believe, almost $3 million in 50 years? The table below assumes that the first $360 you have saved is deposited immediately, and left to compound annually.

GROWTH OF $360 A YEAR, COMPOUNDING ANNUALLY*

Years	5%	10%	15%
5	$ 2,089	$ 2,418	$ 2,791
10	4,754	6,311	8,406
20	12,499	22,681	42,412
30	25,114	65,140	179,984
40	45,662	175,267	736,543
50	79,134	460,908	2,988,135

*Before tax

If you think of every dollar as a "worker dollar," you'll soon find that your spending—and savings—habits will change. You'll be paying attention to waste. Every dollar wasted is one less dollar working for you. You'll pay attention to time, as the older you are, the better the return you'll need to make in order to reach your financial goals. Finally, you'll pay attention to your investment mix. Choosing the right combination of investments and their yields can make a big difference to your dollars' performance.

Most people will start accumulating capital for their investment portfolio with a savings account and then move their investments to a fixed-term, fixed-income deposit—such as a Canada Savings Bonds or Guaranteed Investment Certificate—once minimum deposit levels are reached. For this reason, it is important to manage the term of the deposit as well as its interest rate.

Your interest rate can have a dramatic effect on your capital appreciation. The following chart illustrates what will happen to $1,000 invested over a period of years at a variety of different rates.

Investing your money with a keen eye for the rate of return is, therefore, important. Take an interest-bearing investment, such as a Guaranteed Investment Certificate, for example, compounding annually.

VALUE OF $1,000 GIC COMPOUNDING ANNUALLY
P.S.: Show this to your 15 year old

Years	3%	5%	8%	10%	12%
1	$1,030	$1,050	$1,080	$1,100	$1,120
3	1,093	1,158	1,260	1,331	1,405
5	1,159	1,276	1,469	1,611	1,762
10	1,344	1,629	2,159	2,594	3,106
20	1,806	2,653	4,661	6,721	9,646
30	2,427	4,322	10,063	17,449	29,960
40	3,262	7,040	21,725	45,259	93,051
50	$4,384	$11,467	$46,902	$117,391	$289,002

The numbers tell the story! The higher the interest rate, the faster dollars multiply.

To smooth out the highs and lows of our economic cycles, mix the length of your investment terms. Short-term and long-term investments that mature at different points in the economic cycle will level out the consequences of interest rate fluctuations.

In short, it always pays to be hawkish about interest rates. These decisions about rate and term will have a significant impact on your standard of living later on in life. In fact, the less time you have to reach your goals, the more you should be concerned about your investment's overall performance.

CHAPTER 14
The Relationship between Time and Money

How do you invest money wisely? How do you earn the most with your disposable dollars? Much of your success in attaining your goals will depend on the relationship between time and amount of money invested, as well as risk and return. The less time and money you have now, the more emphasis you'll have to place on rates of return and related risk.

BASIC RULES FOR WEALTH ACCUMULATION

You have seen that it doesn't take much to translate $1.00 into many dollars over a lifetime. Let's assume your goal is to accumulate $500,000 before you reach age 65. You are 25 years old today. That gives you 40 years to reach your goal. How much will you have to save? This will largely depend on the type of investment you own and its return. Let's assume you possess interest-bearing investments only, that earn an average rate of 6 per cent, compounding annually. The returns below are calculated before taxes are paid, and assume that the first deposit is made one period from today.

> **MONEY MANAGEMENT TIP 23**
>
> Understand the significance of time. You will need better overall returns to reach the same goals if you start saving at age 45 instead of age 25. Start investing early.

GOAL: ACCUMULATION OF $500,000 AT AGE 65*
At Compound Interest Rate of 6%, How Much Do I Have to Save?

Age	Years	Compounding Frequency	In a Year	Every Month
25	40	Annual	$ 3,231	$ 269.23
35	30	Annual	6,324	527.04
45	20	Annual	13,592	1,132.69
55	10	Annual	37,934	3,161.17

* Note: Returns are before tax.

This example also illustrates that it is much more manageable to save your projected retirement capital when you are younger, because you have more time on your side.

> **MONEY MANAGEMENT TIP 24**
>
> Understand, how compounding—the earning of interest on reinvested interest—can increase investment results.

Here's how compounding interest—payment of interest on reinvested interest—will help you. The example below also illustrates the difference various rates of return can make. Assume your goal is to maximize the return on your hard-earned savings of $1,000 this year.

PRINCIPAL INVESTED: $1,000 / COMPOUNDING FREQUENCY: ANNUAL*			
Years	4%	8%	10%
5	$1,217	$1,469	$1,611
10	$1,480	$2,159	$2,594
15	$1,801	$3,172	$4,177
20	$2,191	$4,661	$6,727
25	$2,666	$6,848	$10,835

*Note: Returns are before tax.

Conclusions

- The longer you let your money compound the more dramatic the affect of compounding.
- Over a period of 25 years, you'll accumulate more than four times as much at an interest rate of 10 per cent as at a rate of 4 per cent.

> **MONEY MANAGEMENT TIP 25**
>
> Understand the effects of compounding frequency. The more often your institution pays you interest on your investment during the year, the faster your money will multiply.

The shorter the time line, the more important it is that you seek investments that will pay you interest as frequently as possible. Compare the chart below with the previous one.

PRINCIPAL INVESTED: $1,000 / COMPOUNDING FREQUENCY: SEMI-ANNUAL			
Years	4%	8%	10%
5	$1,219	$1,480	$1,629
10	1,486	2,191	2,653
15	1,811	3,243	4,322
20	2,208	4,801	7,040
25	2,692	7,107	11,467

Note: Returns are before tax.

A simple decision like choosing semi-annual compounding over annual compounding investment puts extra dollars in your pocket, without any more time and effort on your part!

The examples above deal with a one-time investment of $1,000 and its growth over a period of years. If you keep adding new capital to your savings every year, the multiplier effect of compound interest is even more dramatic.

PRINCIPAL INVESTED: $1,000 NOW AND THEN AGAIN AT THE START OF EACH YEAR Compounding Frequency: Semi-Annual			
Years	4%	8%	10%
5	$ 5,640	$ 6,366	$ 6,764
10	12,514	15,788	17,783
15	20,895	29,736	35,731
20	31,110	50,382	64,967
25	43,563	80,943	112,588
35	77,246	193,145	316,514

Your original principal of $25,000 invested over 25 years almost doubles at 4 per cent return, and more than quadruples at a 10 per cent return. Over 35 years, your original principal of $35,000 multiplies almost 10 times at a return of 10 per cent. It is easy to see that time and rate of return are critical factors in your eventual wealth accumulation.

This phenomenon of compounding can work wonders, but what do you do if you need two or three more times that much to reach your goals for financial independence? How much of a rate of return will you need?

MONEY MANAGEMENT TIP 26

Understand how to estimate growth. How long will it take you to double or triple your money? To compute this quickly, apply the following rules.

THE RULE OF 72

How Long Will It Take to Double My Money?
Method: Divide 72 by Your Rate of Return

Rate	Length of Time to Double
2%	36 years
3%	24 years
4%	18 years
5%	14.4 years
6%	12 years
7%	10.3 years
8%	9 years
9%	8 years
10%	7.2 years
11%	6.5 years
12%	6 years

THE RULE OF 113

How Long Will It Take to Triple My Money?
Method: Divide 113 by Your Rate of Return

Rate	Length of Time to Triple
3%	37.67 years
6%	18.83 years
9%	12.55 years
12%	9.42 years

This should mean that if you invest $55,000 today at 6 per cent, you will double your money in 12 years to $110,000. Alternatively, if you have $90,000 on deposit today, earning an interest rate of 6 per cent, your money will triple in 18.83 years.

How accurate are these estimates? It turns out that the answer depends on whether your investment is compounding annually or semi-annually, as the following chart illustrates.

ACCURACY TEST: RULE OF 72
How Long Will It Take Me to Double My Money?
Capital: $55,000

	Today	In 6 years	In 12 Years	In 18 Years
Rule of 72:	$55,000	$110,000	$220,000	$440,000
Semi-Annual Compounding:	Actual	$110,670	$222,690	$448,100
Annual Compounding:	Actual	$108,560	$214,279	$422,948

In summary, you must seek out the best returns for the amount of time and money you have available to reach your financial objectives. At its simplest level, this means striving for the best interest rates and fixed-income investments, choosing compounding investments where this makes sense, maximizing opportunities for compounding frequencies and diversification of maturity terms.

However, your asset mix is also important in determining investment returns. Once you start to diversify your portfolio, you must possess a better understanding of your investment product options and their risk factors.

CHAPTER 15
Entry into the Capital Marketplace

Once you have accumulated $500 or $1,000 in your savings account, most institutions will have a type of "debt instrument"—such as a term deposit or GIC that you can move the money into. At certain times of the year (October-November, for example) other investment opportunities arise such as the purchase of Canada Savings Bonds. This type of investment offers a steady, guaranteed growth over a set period of time in which there is virtually no risk of losing your principal. These bonds even allow for investments as low as $100.

> **MONEY MANAGEMENT TIP 27**
> As soon as you have accumulated minimum deposit amounts, move them into higher interest-bearing vehicles.

In the "investment or capital marketplace," there are many different types of investment vehicles designed to give you an opportunity to put your money to work, at various rates of return. Such investment vehicles are often referred to as "securities." A security can be either a certificate that shows you have loaned your money to the issuer of the certificate (such as a bond) or a certificate that shows you have purchased part ownership of the issuer's company (such as a share of common stock).

The types of investments that are available in return for your capital can be classified into three main groupings.

TYPES OF INVESTMENTS AVAILABLE

1. *Cash Equivalents*: money market funds*, Treasury Bills (T-Bills).

2. *Fixed-Income Securities*: usually bonds or other debt instruments that pay a stated rate of income, such as federal, provincial or municipal bonds, corporate bonds, Guaranteed Investment Certificates (GICs), preferred stocks, life insurance policies with fixed cash values, certain mutual funds or foreign bonds.

3. *Variable-Income Securities*: this can include common stock, real estate, business interests, commodities, art, precious metals, tax shelters.

You become a participant in Canada's "Capital Marketplace" as soon as you open a savings account, buy a Canada Savings Bond or a mutual fund. You lend your money to a party, usually a government or public/private company. The Capital Marketplace is composed of:

1. *Financial institutions*, such as banks and trust companies.

2. *Stock exchanges*, such as the Toronto or Vancouver Stock Exchange.

3. *Investment dealers*: a firm or individual who may act as the owner of new securities it underwrites in addition to selling other securities.

4. *Stock brokers*: a firm or individual who acts as an agent in buying and selling securities in return for a commission.

5. *Investors:* people who wish to buy securities for cash.

---

* Short-term credit instruments.

In making a decision about where to invest your disposable income, there are eight considerations you must take into account, a few of which have been introduced in previous chapters.

Elements of an Investment

1. Security (type of risk exposure on principal and income).
2. Return on capital (interest, dividends, capital gains, business profits).
3. Capital Appreciation (an increase in the value of your principal).
4. Liquidity and Marketability (How easy is it to get your cash out?)
5. Diversification (Do I have too many eggs in one basket?)
6. Management Requirements (Canada Savings Bonds vs. apartment block).
7. Timing (successful buying and selling).
8. Tax Considerations (keeping larger after-tax returns).

How important is each element to your investment portfolio? Which have top priority? To answer this, you will need to look at a series of factors in your own life:

Factors in Choosing the Best Investment

- your age
- the state of your health
- the number of dependants you have
- your level of income
- your existing savings
- your sources of income
- your total financial obligations
- your tax bracket
- your current asset mix
- your attitude towards risk.

MONEY MANAGEMENT TIP 28

Match your age with the type and level of risk in your investment portfolio. Price fluctuations, uncertain interest rates, risk of corporate default or loss of purchasing power must be anticipated.

In analyzing where to place your money, know the risks associated with your decision and remember this old adage:

"Behold the turtle . . . he only makes progress when he sticks his neck out."

James B. Conant

CHAPTER 16
Risk and Reward

In the investment marketplace, there is a definite pattern to the elements of risk and reward: **The Higher the Reward, the Bigger the Risk**

Risk is your potential for loss. Before you make decisions about where to place your capital, you should have a good handle on your "risk tolerance level." Probably the best way to gauge this is to consider whether you'll be able to sleep at night after you've made your decision. This will largely depend on what resources you have to fall back on in case your investment strategies stall or fail outright.

How does risk arise? Potential for loss fluctuates according to the changing events in the marketplace, including:

1. *A change in economic activity:* increases or declines in business profits, housing starts and other economic activities in response to market conditions, can cause "Credit Risks."
2. *A change in stock market conditions:* increases or declines in the price of securities in response to their level of trading, or the level of trading overall. This is also called "Market Risk."
3. *A change in interest rates* or "Interest Rate Risk:" increases and decreases in profit levels throughout the marketplace.
4. *A change in market prices* or "Purchasing Power Risk," may change the future purchasing power of your investment.
5. *A change in political direction* or "Political Risk:" uncertainty in a government's taxation and economic policies affects the marketplace.

As you can see, the constant changes in the world around us can have a very dramatic affect on the performance of your investments and safety of your principal. It is, therefore, important to develop a specific investment strategy that encompasses your values and goals, as well as acknowledging the various cycles of the economy as a whole.

These are heady concepts, particularly for a beginner. However, there is a way to make sense of it all. It begins with an organized approach to your financial portfolio.

All investments contain some level of risk.

Levels of Risk in an Investment

Is common stock riskier than a Canada Savings Bond? Everyone knows that your principal is guaranteed in the latter, but not the former. However, CSBs are not entirely without risk—interest rate risk, or risk of higher taxation will affect how much of a return eventually lands in your own pocket.

Investments can encompass degrees of risk—from moderate to risky, for example—as a result of volatility in the marketplace or poor management. You may wish to discuss the fluctuating risk levels of your potential investments with your investment advisor.

One way you can inform and protect yourself from risk is to become aware of the "Ratings" of your potential investments. In Canada, we have bond rating services that assess the quality of certain investments. Such an assessment can tell you much about a company in which you are planning to invest. The Dominion Bond Rating Service is an example of such a service. This company rates issuers of commercial paper, term debt and preferred shares so that investors can be provided with an assessment of the credit quality of their potential investments.

The company will point out that a credit rating is not to be construed as a buy/sell recommendation. The rating, for instance, will not evaluate market risks which result from fluctuations in interest rates or exchange rates; nor will it evaluate risk in trading liquidity.

Because credit ratings will fluctuate, an investor must be careful to look beyond the rating in some cases. Is the change in credit quality the result of structural changes or cyclical changes? The Dominion Bond Rating Service will analyze four main topic areas:

1. Past, present and projected future earnings.
2. Past, present and projected future balance sheets.
3. Subjective factors such as size, industry conditions and management experience/competence.
4. Indenture (contractual) provisions.

Here are some examples. If you are buying short-term negotiable debt securities issued by a corporation with terms of a few days up to a year—commercial paper—you might find the following ratings classifications useful. Also following are the rating scales for long-term debt and preferred shares.

Rating Scale: Commercial Paper and Short-Term Debt

R-1 Prime Quality. The company's ability to repay current liabilities is excellent. Profitability is reasonable and stable, and the ability to liquidate is excellent. Alternative funding exists.

R-2 Medium Grade. Liquidity is not as strong. Alternative sources of liquidity are strong, the size of the company affects flexibility, and profitability trends are less favourable and not as stable.

R-3 Speculative Grade. Liquidity ratios are below average, alternative sources are questionable and earnings are very unstable. Overall profitability looks low.

Rating Scale: Bonds and Long-Term Debt

AAA Highest Credit Quality. The highest order of protection is afforded to principal and interest. Earnings are relatively stable and the outlook for future profitability is extremely good. Extremely strong liquidity factors.

AA Superior Quality. Protection of principal and interest is high; very little difference from AAA.

A Upper Medium Grade. Protection of principal and interest is substantial but less than AA. These companies are more susceptible to adverse economic conditions and are affected by economic cycle changes.

BBB Medium Grade. Protection of principal and interest is adequate but the entity is susceptible to economic cycles or there is a presence of other adversities.

BB Lower Medium Grade. Mildly speculative, the degree of protection of principal and interest is uncertain, particularly during recessionary periods; size of company is usually small.

B Speculative Quality. There is uncertainty in the ability to pay principal and interest in the future, especially in a recessionary period.

CCC Highly Speculative. There is danger of default on principal and interest.

CC   In Default, of either principal or interest.

C   Lowest Grade. These bonds have lower liquidation values and rank than CC bonds.

Rating Scale: Preferred Shares

Pfd-1 Superior Credit Quality. These shares have strong earnings and balance sheets. Their bond rating is usually AA or better.

Pfd-2 Upper Medium Grade Credit Quality. The earnings, balance sheet and coverage ratios are not as strong as Pfd-1; bond ratings are usually A.

Pfd-3 Medium Grade Credit Quality. These companies usually have BBB bond ratings.

Pfd-4 Lower Medium Grade Credit Quality. Creditworthiness is somewhat speculative and bonds are usually rated as a BB category.

Pfd-5 Speculative Credit Quality. Bond ratings are in the B or lower category.

"D" This category indicates that preferred shares are not paying dividends.

"low" A low grade is generally allocated to "junior" preferred shares and non-cumulative preferred shares.

Investors may also wish to ask their investment advisor about ratings through the Canadian Bond Rating Service. This company is also engaged in credit assessment of the various Canadian issuers seeking to raise finds in Canadian and international capital markets. It will also rate private placements.

The eight areas analyzed by the CBRS include:
1. Economic environment.
2. Industry analysis.
3. Management, history and forecasting record.
4. Accounting policies and procedures.
5. Cash flow and earnings.
6. Capital structure and asset protection.
7. Financial policies and funding alternatives.
8. Indenture provisions and loan covenants.

The best way to accumulate both income from your investments and growth, with a minimum of risk, is to determine a balanced mix of investments that best suit your needs according to your resources, age and objectives.

> **MONEY MANAGEMENT TIP 29**
> Find out as much as you can about the risk levels of the investments you wish to use.

CHAPTER 17 Debt Securities

When you have extra cash—disposable income—that's left over after you cover all of your personal living expenses—you will be seeking the most advantageous ways to put your extra money to work for you. When you invest your money, there are two primary types of securities you can acquire: *Debt Securities* and *Ownership or Equity Securities*. Ownership securities—investments in which you become a part owner of the firm—will be discussed in the next chapter.

When you acquire a debt security, you will be contracting to lend out your money to a variety of borrowers in the capital or financial marketplace, and they in turn will pay you for the use of your money in their enterprises. These borrowers—corporations or governments, for example—will give you an I.O.U. or certificate in exchange for your money. This certificate is a contract that will describe the interest rate you'll be earning. The length of time the money will be held by the borrower, or the term, is also established in the contract. Debt securities are sometimes known as "fixed-income securities." Fixed-income securities can include notes, bonds, debentures and preferred stocks.

PRIMARY AND SECONDARY MARKETS

When a debt instrument, such as a bond, is newly issued and sold directly from the issuer to an investor, we are said to be trading in the "primary market." However, if we wish to resell our investment before maturity, we can do so in a "secondary market." This is where investors buy and sell securities among themselves.

This secondary market gives the bond market more "liquidity"—the ability to turn investments quickly back into cash.

This is a very important concept, because activity in the secondary markets can affect your income and your tax status in different ways. For example, you might be holding onto a bond that carries a higher interest rate than other securities in the marketplace today. In that case, you could probably sell it at a value that exceeds its face value and interest components. You would incur a "capital gain" on the increase in value. However, the opposite can happen, too. If you sell the bond for less than what you paid for it, a capital loss will result. (The tax consequences of these activities are discussed in detail in Part 3.)

Interest rates have a big bearing on the value of your bonds. If interest rates rise, your bond prices in the secondary market will generally go down. But, when interest rates fall, bond prices will generally rise.

CORPORATE AND GOVERNMENT DEBT

It is important to know why borrowers are seeking your capital before you invest. For example, corporations will pay you for the right to use your money to finance expansion or improvements. The reasons they are contracting with you is because their revenues are otherwise insufficient to pay for these plans. However, their bond issues are usually secured with specific assets that can be liquidated.

Government debt, which is incurred to finance capital projects such as the building of bridges or schools, or operating deficits, is not usually secured with specific assets. Security is considered to be the ability to tax individuals and corporations. These taxes pay for the debt instruments.

As previously discussed in Chapter 16, investors can take some of the risk out of their investment decisions by consulting ratings of the various bond rating services. These ratings are sold to your investment dealer, who can update you. This will tell you something about the quality of a bond you are considering.

The Bank of Canada is the federal government's agent for handling the distribution of all its debt instruments. The Bank of Canada will offer its bonds to investment dealers and banks at a discount from the retail price. These intermediaries sell the bonds to the public.

In Canada, both provincial and municipal governments also issue bonds. Bonds that mature within three years are considered to be "short term"; three to 10 years "medium term"; and more than 10 years, "long term."

To make a decision about where to place your money, it helps to understand the characteristics of bonds and other fixed-income securities that are available in the marketplace. The main difference between a bond and debenture, for example, is that a debenture is an unsecured debt; that is, there are no assets in place to back the debenture. However, certain other government bonds can have those same characteristics and still be called "bonds."

BOND COSTS AND YIELD

The interest rate on the bond or debenture you buy can be paid in a variety of intervals, but generally every six months. With the exception of Canada Savings Bonds and certain provincial bond issues, most bonds traded in the marketplace are acquired at a value that includes accrued interest. A buyer will typically pay this accrued interest to the seller at the time of purchase, and then receive it and any additional accrued interest at a subsequent sale. Any interest paid on acquisition is a deductible carrying charge on your tax return; subsequent accrued interest earned is reported as income as of the next interest payment date or upon disposition of the bond.

When you sell your bond, you may also incur a capital gain or loss if your proceeds of disposition exceed the bond's adjusted cost base, or what you can acquire the bond for (including commissions). Therefore, to calculate the yield of your investment, your broker will factor in both the accrued interest and potential gain or loss.

When you buy a bond at "par" value, you are receiving it for its face value plus accrued interest. In this case, your return would be higher than it would be by earning interest only. If you pay more than par, you have acquired the bond at a "premium." In such cases, your yield will be lower than the interest rate on your coupon. Therefore, when you speak of a bond yield, you are asking your representative to describe the real rate of return after purchase price, time to maturity, capital gain or loss, and stated interest rate.

Ask your investment advisor to determine whether any of the following investments should be included in your investment portfolio.

> **MONEY MANAGEMENT TIP 30**
> Familiarize yourself with the various debt obligations you may choose to invest in, and how their accrual yields differ.

TYPES OF FIXED-INCOME SECURITIES

Canada Savings Bonds   These are debt instruments of the federal government with a difference from most other bonds—they can be cashed at any time. Interest will be paid on each redemption only if a minimum holding period of three months has been met. Once acquired, you cannot transfer ownership of the CSB to anyone else. They are usually sold in the beginning of November every year, and can be purchased on a payroll plan for a set carrying charge that is tax deductible. Interest is paid annually on regular interest bonds or can accrue and compound as "C" bonds or compounding bonds.

Commercial Paper   This refers to short-term debt securities that are issued by corporations with holding terms of a few days or months, or up to one year.

Convertible Bond or Debenture   A type of security that may be exchanged for common stock of the same company, at the discretion of the company. The terms for conversion are set out in the original acquisition.

Coupons   These are the parts of a bond that can be clipped and presented for interest payment on or after the bond's due date. The amount of interest to be paid is generally specified on the coupon.

Cumulative Preferred Stock   This is preferred stock whose terms stipulate that unpaid dividends owing to the investor must accumulate and be paid out before any further dividends are distributed to common shareholders.

Debenture   A debt obligation issued by a government or corporation that is unsecured by assets.

Extendible Bond   Such bonds allow the bondholder to receive the right to keep the bond for a number of additional years beyond its normal maturity date. These terms are outlined in the certificate.

Guaranteed Investment Certificate   This type of debt instrument is sold at its face value at an interest rate and term that are set in advance. It can be either redeemable in a certain period or non-redeemable. GICs are defined as "deposit instruments" which differ from a bond because they are usually issued by a bank or trust company, which uses the money in the same way it would if you put it in a savings account.

Income Bond While your principal is fully repayable, this type of bond will pay interest only when and if it is earned. Unpaid interest can accumulate to maturity.

Mortgage-Backed Securities These investments are best described as a group or "pool" of home mortgages. They are usually sold in units with specific terms. The issuer of the securities will buy a large number of residential mortgages, a share of which each investor owns. The investor receives interest and principal payments each month, and in addition may receive income from mortgage pre-payments. These securities trade in the bond markets, usually at current interest rates.

Non-Cumulative Preferred Stock Dividends that are missed will not be accumulated for the investor.

Note A promise to pay you back the money you have lent, but on an unsecured basis.

Retractable Security With this type of investment, you (the lender) may be granted the option to redeem the security on a stated date prior to maturity.

Serial Bond A bond or debenture in which a set amount of principal becomes due and payable each year.

Strip Bonds These popular investments are generally a high-quality government bond from which some or all of the interest coupons have been detached or "stripped." These coupons are sold separately (as is the principal certificate). You may trade them before maturity, but in such cases you are subject to the pricing of the marketplace, which can be risky. This is so because the coupon you acquire has "zero coupons" attached to it. Each coupon is acquired at a discount, and there is no actual "interest" payment. However, a compounded rate of return based on the par value and the amount of time to maturity is calculated and these returns are reported as accrued interest annually on your tax return.

Treasury Bills A short-term government debt obligation issued in denominations of usually $10,000 or more. The difference between the discount price at which a T-bill is acquired and par value is treated as interest on the income tax return.

Warrants These are certificates that give the holder the right to purchase securities in the company at a set price and usually with a time clause.

CHAPTER 18 The Stock Market

When you participate in the stock market, you are taking advantage of the opportunity of acquiring (or disposing of) a share of the company in which you are investing. As a shareholder, you will have the potential to share in the profits and acquire wealth as the company increases in value.

Why do companies sell off a portion of their shares? As companies evolve, new capital is needed to continue growth and development. As we have seen in the last chapter, debt instruments may be issued to finance such growth. When you become a creditor of a firm or government by holding a debt instrument, such as a bond, you must be paid back your principal together with the agreed upon interest at a specified term. If the company to whom you have lent money fails, you would usually have a good claim on the assets of the company.

When you become a shareholder, you own a part of the company you invested in and you have specific rights, too.

RIGHTS OF A SHAREHOLDER

- You have the right to share in the profits of the company.
- You have the right to influence growth by voting at the annual shareholders' meeting.
- In case of business failure, your rights on the assets of the company fall behind those of any creditors.
- You may have rights to special features that allow you to buy or sell shares in the future.

When you buy a share of a company, you will not be paid any interest because you have not lent any money. However, you might be paid a "dividend," which is an after-tax distribution of profits of the firm. (See Part 3 for taxation of dividends.)

As well, you have the opportunity to capitalize on the growth of the original value of the firm over time. If that happens, you will make a profit on the sale of those shares sometime in the future. This increase in value of the shares over the price you paid for them is called a "capital gain." A capital gain (or loss) will only occur when there is a disposition of your ownership interest or "equity" in the company.

However, if the value of its shares should fall and, if you decide or are forced to sell, you may have to do so at an amount less than what you invested in the firm. The difference between the original cost of the shares and your lower disposition proceeds is called a "capital loss." The tax consequences of these events are discussed in more detail in Part 3.

Shareholders also carry the full burden of risk of losing their investment should there be business failure. Bank loans, bonds and debentures, and creditors must all be paid off before the shareholders receive anything.

The stock market consists primarily in the trading of stock from corporations. Because governments don't generally have assets to sell, they usually raise money through the bond market.

HOW DO NEW SHARES COME TO THE MARKETPLACE?

A new company can raise money in several ways:
- the original owners may invest capital privately, if the company is privately held
- the company may borrow money from the bank
- it might reinvest the profits or "retained earnings"
- it might issue debt instruments such as bonds
- it might issue shares in the company either privately or to the public, in order to raise necessary capital and award interest costs.

Timing has much to do with the type of financing a company may choose. In a recessionary period, for example, interest rates are lower and borrowing from an institution, if possible, may be more attractive than issuing shares in the company. It might be more difficult to raise money through a share offering if stock prices are low. This could affect whether or not the company can raise the capital it needs from the sale of shares.

If a company raises money through a share offering, it will avoid paying interest on the money raised, which should affect its profitability in a positive way. In fact, unlike the required repayment provisions of a loan, the company does not have to make plans for repayment of the investment of the shareholders. Nor is it required to pay a dividend. However, if the company is profitable, issuing shares may be expensive for two reasons. First, dividends are paid out to shareholders on after-tax earnings and there is no tax deduction for this payment. Second, in making the share offering, the company does give up something important—ownership.

When a company decides to offer ownership in its firm as a means to raise capital, it must develop a "new offering" that is usually "underwritten" by an investment dealer. This is a formal agreement between the company and an investment dealer to acquire the shares for resale purposes.

When a "public offering" is made, the company must prepare a "prospectus." This is a document that describes the new securities in detail, their price and type, and gives detailed information about the company. A "preliminary prospectus" must be filed with the provincial securities administrator. This is a document you should review with your investment advisor, if you are considering investing in a new offering.

The investment dealer may decide to purchase the offering entirely for resale to investors by acquiring the securities before a preliminary prospectus is filed. The company is guaranteed a certain amount of money in this instance, and need not take back any unsold shares. The dealer, who may acquire the company's shares either alone or as part of a "bank group," may resell some or all of the shares or keep some in "inventory."

The investment dealer may also act only as an agent in selling the securities to investors in some instances.

In general, when the stock exchange is used to raise capital for companies, the seller is not the company who issued the stock but someone trading on the "secondary market"—someone who either bought the stock from the company or another investor. Therefore, if the company has "gone public," it has arranged for its shares to be listed and traded on the stock exchange or public marketplace. It does not itself profit from increases in valuation of the shares as they are traded from investor to investor, but fluctuations in the value of the shares will have a bearing on the company's decision to make another share offering in the future. A good time to do this would, of course, be when the value of the shares is up.

A company can, by the way, purchase some of its own shares. It may do so for subsequent resale, for example. This is called a "buy-back."

PRIMARY ROLES OF PUBLIC STOCK EXCHANGES

- The stock exchange makes it possible for investors to get their money out of a firm.
- Investors are able to choose from a large variety of stocks in different companies.
- Investors can buy new issues, or shares that have been in existence for a long period of time.
- Investors can buy or sell shares whenever they want, subject to the wants and needs of the marketplace.

- Companies can capitalize on the success of one share issue by bringing forward another one.

TYPES OF STOCK EXCHANGES

Did you know that in Canada, we have a number of different stock exchanges? We hear daily about the major ones—the Toronto Stock Exchange or the Montreal Stock Exchange, for example. However, we have smaller exchanges: the Vancouver, Winnipeg and Alberta Stock Exchanges are examples. These exchanges feature many new companies or "juniors." Often new resource companies, such as oil and gas companies, or lumber and mining companies, are listed here.

Junior stock exchanges are generally "venture capital specialists." Because they help get new companies off the ground, and the companies themselves often do not have a track record, the stocks on these exchanges are often riskier in nature. However, this doesn't always mean there is less risk with the companies listed on the larger exchanges.

HOW TO TRADE ON THE STOCK EXCHANGE

Trading takes place through a stock broker at an "Investment Dealer." This person will place an order for stock for you, and earns a commission when the sales transaction is completed. You must place your orders for stocks you wish to acquire through a "member" of the stock exchange who owns a "seat" there. This will generally be stock brokerage firms and investment dealers. To own a seat, the firm must meet certain admission standards for membership.

The stock market is like a big auction. The price of the stock will be determined by how many buyers there are for that item in the marketplace. Trading can be done on the stock market floor itself or, more prevalent today, electronically through a network of computers.

When an order is placed on your behalf, it is called a buy order or a "bid." Investors who wish to sell stock put in a sell order or an "ask."

You may also become aware of an "Over the Counter Market." This is a market that sells unlisted shares. Stocks and bonds can be acquired by auction, as well as by negotiation.

> **MONEY MANAGEMENT TIP 31**
> Familiarize yourself with the working of the stock market to maximize your participation in the process of buying and selling shares.

CHAPTER 19
Common Stock

There are two types of stock that can be acquired on the stock exchanges: common and preferred. In this chapter, we will discuss common stock.

When you own common stock, you become a part owner of the company. As well, you have one vote for each share owned in the selection of the management of the firm. At annual meetings, the shareholders will elect directors to represent them. If and when the company turns a profit, you may have a right to some of the profits. The board of directors may declare a dividend, which is paid out of the company's after-tax earnings. This decision is based on current profit and cash flow levels, as well as a look to the future capital needs of the company. Dividends are usually paid to shareholders quarterly, but can be paid semi-annually or annually. When you acquire stock of a company, you may be offered a whole variety of other rights and options during the course of your time with the company as part-owner. To help you decipher the meaning of these events when they arise, consider the following:

Stock Dividends A company's board of directors may wish to declare a dividend, but anticipate that cash reserves will be required for expansion or other activities. They may issue the dividend in the form of extra stock instead of cash.

Rights Shareholders of a company may also have special rights to acquire additional shares of that company, in direct proportion to the number of shares owned. If such a "rights issue" is made, the price at which individual shareholders can acquire more shares is usually lower than the market price of the shares; in addition, the shareholders must exercise their rights within a given time frame. These "rights" in themselves become a marketable investment that can be traded on the stock exchange. However, in the period of time before the rights become tradeable, shareholders will usually have one right for each share held. In this period, the rights are known as "Cum Rights." The period of time after this, until such time as the offering expires, is called the "Ex Rights" period.

Warrants Sometimes, to make a new offering more attractive, securities (usually preferred shares or debentures) come with "warrants." These are a type of certificate that give the shareholder the right to purchase additional stock in a specified time frame at a set price. This can be very valuable, particularly if you have acquired the stock at below the market price in the first place.

Options If you acquire an option, you have the ability to sell your security at today's price at some date in the future. This is called a "put option." A "call option," on the other hand, allows you to buy stock at today's prices at a specified time in the future. These options afford you some protection if used properly.

Futures Futures are contracts that obligate you to buy or sell a security at a set time and price in the future.

Note: In general terms, warrants, options and futures can be riskier than the acquisition of the stocks because of their complexity. Speak to your investment dealer about them.

How can you judge which stocks you should invest in? To make an informed decision, you should consult with your investment dealer or advisor and learn to look for the companies that will help you meet your investment objectives.

MONEY MANAGEMENT TIP 32

Diversify your portfolio as a hedge against risk. Learn to read the performance statistics of stocks you hold in the financial dailies.

HOW TO READ THE STOCK TABLES
Source: *The Globe and Mail*

1	2	3	4	5	6	7	8	9	10	11	12
Footnotes	52-Week High Low	Stock Name	Trading Symbol	Div	High	Low	Close	Change	Vol	Yield	P/E Ratio
da	$28\frac{1}{8}$ $25\frac{3}{8}$	Altamax Co.	XYZ	—	$26\frac{5}{8}$	$26\frac{1}{2}$	$26\frac{1}{2}$	—	.10	8.49	—

Our fictitious Altamax Co. is shown on a typical stock table. The format above is taken from *The Globe and Mail* stock tables.

Here is the meaning of the information.

1. **Footnotes:** If your stock line begins with an up arrow (↑), it means the stock has reached a new 52-week high. A down arrow (↓) means

it has reached a new 52-week low. Other common footnotes are as follows:
a—a spin-off company has been distributed
n—indicates a new issue or new listing on the stock exchange
s—the stock has recently split or a stock dividend has been paid
x or xd—the stock is trading "ex dividend" or without dividends
xc—a capital gains distribution will be paid to the current owner
da—this means there is a dividend in arrears
j—this stock is subject to special rules
nr—a non-voting share
rc—in bankruptcy or receivership
rs—a resource stock
rv—shareholders' voting rights are restricted

2. **52-Week High/Low:** This column indicates both the highest and the lowest price achieved by the stock in the past 52 weeks.
3. **The Stock Name:** You'll often find these names abbreviated in the tables.
4. **The Trading Symbol:** This is the symbol used for the company on the stock exchange. The symbol may have a suffix:
   .PR means a preferred share
   .S means stock is subject to regulation
   .UN means a unit
   .W means when issued
   .WT means a warrant (right to purchase other securities)
5. **Dividend:** This describes the annual dividend value, if any.
6. **High:** The highest trading price of the day or highest asking price for stocks that did not trade.
7. **Low:** The lowest trading price of the day, or lowest bid offered.
8. **Close:** The price at which the stock closed on this particular day.
9. **Change:** This is the change between today's closing price and yesterday's closing price.
10. **Volume:** This figure is shown in units of 100. If you see 10, for example, it means 10 x 100, or 1,000, shares were traded.
11. **Yield:** This is the dividend yield. The dividend is divided by the current market price.
12. **P/E Ratio:** This is the current stock price divided by the company's earnings per share from operations of the past 12 months.

Your favourite business page will describe in detail the abbreviated information contained in the stock pages.

CHAPTER 20
What to Look for in Acquiring Common Stock

When you invest your money in a common stock, you are making several decisions at once. You might be acquiring the possibility of earning both income and capital appreciation. Your decision to invest in a common stock should be well matched to your overall financial objectives.

The key questions you should be presenting to your broker for discussion before you invest are the following:

1. What type of industry is the company in?
2. How does the company compare in performance to other companies in the same industry?
3. How is the company performing in the current economic climate?
4. What are the short-term profitability prospects?
5. Why is the long-term prospect for capital appreciation good?

When you are investing your money in the stock market, it is reasonable to set some kind of goal for a return on your investment—let's say one to two years. In order to accomplish this, you must have some sense of how a particular industry is evolving and try to pick companies that are leading in their industry. By watching business evolutions within an industry, you can better diversify your investment portfolio to balance risk and reward.

You might also wish to choose corporations that are in different growth cycles. For example, you may wish to select some that are developing new products or services, or you may be keen on relatively new but established companies whose sales are increasing at a fast pace, retaining earnings for reinvestment purposes. These companies are typified by aggressive management that is capably maximizing opportunities for future earnings. You'll often hear of these companies as "growth stock."

Your equity mix should also contain stock backed by predictable earnings. Larger, established firms that are still growing fall into such a category. You and your broker might also discuss a "defensive" strategy—a search for stock that is not affected by economic conditions. Such companies provide essential services such as utilities or include food industries, breweries and pharmaceutical industries. Where high and predictable dividends are paid, stocks are referred to as "income stocks" and can include "blue chip" and/or "defensive" stock.

Certain companies are greatly affected by the upturns and downturns of economic cycles. These may include auto, appliances and heavy equipment manufacturers and the forestry industry. Speak to your broker about the timing of acquisitions and dispositions of such stock.

Finally, you may be considering acquiring stock in a company whose products or services are declining in consumer demand for a variety of reasons. Watch their ability to survive acquisitions of other companies, or diversifying product lines.

In short, diversifying your portfolio will help you accomplish a type of balance between short-term risk and long-term reward.

COMPANY PERFORMANCE ANALYSIS

In selecting a specific company for your investment, in a particular industry, a detailed analysis of its operational performance should be considered. You and your investment advisor should look at the following:
- performance over a period of years as per the financial statements of the firm
- quality of management
- plans for product diversification
- research and development initiatives
- merger/acquisition plans
- agreements with suppliers and clients
- labour relations in certain industries
- environmental concerns in certain industries.

> **MONEY MANAGEMENT TIP 33**
>
> Learn to read financial statements in order to analyze the ongoing performance of your equity investments.

We'll look more closely now at the information you can receive from the financial statements.

FINANCIAL STATEMENTS

In analyzing the numbers, look carefully at the following statements:
- The Balance Sheet
- The Income and Expense Statement

- The Retained Earnings Statement
- The Statement of Changes in Financial Position

HOW TO USE INFORMATION FROM FINANCIAL STATEMENTS

The Balance Sheet

This will tell you the financial position of the company at a fixed date. It uses this basic equation: Assets = Liabilities + Owner's Equity. This will reflect all of the activities of the company since it first opened for business. (See Chapter 8 for definitions.)

What will the balance sheet tell you? Well, let's do some analysis. Let's assume a company's balance sheet looks like this:

XYZ COMPANY: BALANCE SHEET			
Assets		**Liabilities**	
Current	$100,000	Current	$ 50,000
Fixed	150,000	Long Term	100,000
		Equity	
		Common Shares	$ 40,000
		Retained Earnings	60,000
Total Assets	$250,000	**Total Liabilities/Equity**	$250,000

- *Can the company meet current obligations?* To answer this question, compute the following:

    What is ratio of current assets to current liabilities?

    $$\frac{\$100,000}{\$ 50,000} = 2:1$$

This means the company is in a position to meet its current obligations. For every dollar in current liabilities, there are two dollars in current assets. If the ratio between current assets and current liabilities is too high, one must question management's ability to maximize the use of capital to produce more profit.

- *How liquid is the company?* To determine how quickly a company can access the funds it needs, vary the above ratio by subtracting inventories on hand from current assets.

- *Does the company have too much debt over the long term?* To determine this, compute the following:

    $$\frac{\text{Total Debt } \$150,000}{\text{Total Debt + Equity } \$250,000} = .6$$

This figure will only have meaning if you compare it to industry standards. What percentage of the total capital investment of the company should be debt without creating instability?

• *What is the price/earnings ratio?* This is one of the most common ways to value a share, and is listed in the daily stock tables.

$$\frac{\text{Current Market Price}}{\text{Earnings per Share}} = \text{Price/ Earnings Ratio}$$

To obtain and use this information, one must look at the earnings of the company on the income statement over a period of time.

Compare your analysis to other companies in the same industry. This ratio is important to investors. If the price/earnings ratio is low, it may mean that the shares are undervalued. It may be a good time to buy from that viewpoint. However, if the price/earnings ratio is high, it may justify paying a higher price for the stock, especially if the company's earnings are expected to grow. Ask your investment advisor about the historical price/earnings ratio and its significance in light of current economic conditions and trends in the marketplace.

The Income and Expense Statement

This statement summarizes the results of business activities. Its basic equation is Revenue – Operating Expenses = Net Profit.

What will an Income and Expense Statement tell you? For an investor, the most important thing is the level of earnings each share brings. Here's a sample:

INCOME AND EXPENSE STATEMENT

Revenue		Expenses		Net Profit
Sales	$250,000	Interest	$ 15,000	$60,000
		Salaries	75,000	
		Overhead	25,000	
		Marketing	30,000	
		Other	45,000	
		Total	**$190,000**	

• To determine the return on your equity, apply the following formula:

$$\frac{\text{Net profit: } \$60,000}{\text{Common shareholder's equity: } \$40,000} = 150\%$$

An excellent return indeed!

- To determine the percentage of net profit to sales:

$$\frac{\text{Net profit: } \$60{,}000}{\text{Total sales: } \$250{,}000} = 24\%$$

How does this compare to other companies in the same industry?

- To determine the ability to pay interest out of income:

$$\frac{\text{Net Profit: } \$60{,}000}{\text{Total Interest Expense: } \$15{,}000} = 4:1$$

Annual interest charges are well covered.

The Retained Earnings Statement

This will tell you how much profit is being reinvested in the company for growth and expansion. It will also indicate potential for income distribution.

The Statement of Changes in Financial Position

This statement will give the investor a good overview of a company's profitability trends and debt management, and its ability to meet market demands over a period of time.

It will also tell you how a company's funds have been used in the period.

As a shareholder, you do not need to know the management of the firm personally to make a judgment about its quality.

It is management's job to run a profitable operation in order for the company to appreciate in value and earn a return on investment for its shareholders. In a corporation, management is responsible to the board of directors, which in turn is responsible to the shareholders. The shareholders may replace this board if the company is not profitable.

This means that the shareholders of the company, by virtue of their voting rights, can in fact control it. As a shareholder, either now or in the future, you may wish to take those voting rights seriously. If you cannot attend a meeting, you may assign your votes to someone who is attending, by returning a "proxy form."

CHAPTER 21: Preferred Shares

When you acquire preferred shares of a corporation, you will have certain privileges that common shareholders will not have. For example, you would be entitled to receive any dividends declared before the common shareholders receive theirs. If the company becomes insolvent, preferred shareholders will have claim to any distribution of remaining assets before common shareholders. It is possible that your approval must be obtained before a new issue of preferreds is made. However, while preferred shareholders participate as part-owners of the company, they usually do not have a vote.

In that preferred shares yield a fixed dividend, they are considered to be fixed-income securities. A dividend is usually payable on a quarterly basis. Such dividends may be cumulative or non-cumulative. If they are cumulative, it means that missed dividend payments accumulate and are paid out before common shareholders receive their dividends. Preferred shareholders will not reap benefits out of the increasing profits of the company over and above this fixed dividend.

There are many different types of preferred shares, offering different features for investors. Ask your investment advisor about the pros and cons of these features before making an investment decision:

Callable Preferreds   These are preferred shares on which the issuer has reserved the right to redeem or "call" them in. A small premium is usually paid to the shareholder when this happens.

Convertible Preferreds   These shares can be converted to common shares at a set price and within a set time. This is advantageous from the investor's viewpoint because he or she benefits from the security features of a preferred share and can still potentially benefit from capital appreciation in the company. The shareholder also is able to avoid paying commission on the conversion to common stock. As well, there are no tax consequences on the conversion at the time of conversion. (Subsequent sales of the converted shares will, of course, be subject to the normal tax rules. See Part 3.) On the downside, these preferreds become "straight preferreds" (see below) when the conversion period is over. In addition, they usually have lower yields than a straight preferred share.

Foreign-pay Preferreds   These preferreds make it possible to receive dividends in a foreign currency. The benefit to the investor comes when the foreign currency rises in relation to the Canadian dollar.

Non-callable Preferreds   These shares cannot be called in for redemption.

Participating Preferreds   These preferreds are issued with rights to share in corporate earnings, in addition to the stipulated dividend rate.

Purchase Funds   These preferreds can be retired through purchases on the open market by the issuer. This would usually happen when prices fall below a stipulated price. It affords some market protection to the investor.

Retractable Preferred Shares   Shareholders in this case can require the issuer to redeem the shares on a specified date and at a specified price. If the retraction date is missed, they become straight preferreds.

Straight Preferreds   These stocks have no special features at all. These investments are usually tied into the interest rates. If interest rates go up, the price of these preferreds usually will go down. The opposite will happen if interest rates fall.

Variable or Floating Rate Preferreds   These preferreds will pay dividends in amounts that will vary with interest rate changes. A "delayed floater" has a feature that will pay a fixed dividend for a period of time and then become a variable rate preferred.

MONEY MANAGEMENT TIP 34

Ask your investment dealer about the types of preferred shares suited to your money management plan's goals, when to acquire them, and in what proportion to your other assets.

Generally, it is better to acquire preferred shares outside of an RRSP, because of the tax advantages extended to dividends (see Part 3).

CHAPTER 22
Mutual Funds and Other "Managed Money"

Decisions, decisions! Some investors prefer just to leave it all to the professionals—and pay for these services.

There are several options for professional money management.

WRAP ACCOUNTS

As an investor, you may wish to leave the intricate decisions of where to invest in the hands of a money management or investment counsel firm. An annual fee, based on a percentage of assets invested is charged to persons who have a relatively large amount of money to invest. The fees will usually drop as the assets multiply in the fund. The idea of the wrap is that the manager has complete discretion to make all investment decisions on your behalf. You would want that manager to have an exact knowledge of your investment objectives and risk tolerance level. Investors with very large portfolios may wish to consider hiring a personal investment manager.

MUTUAL FUNDS

For the average person, mutual fund investment has become a popular way to benefit from diversification opportunities, structured to meet your personal risk tolerance expectations.

When you invest in a mutual fund, you are buying units in the fund's assets. You are making the decision to pool your resources with many other investors who leave the management of the investment choices to professionals. You can continuously buy more units, or you can sell them at the current value. The value depends on the quality of the fund's portfolio.

The "Net Asset Value Per Share" (NAVPS) will determine the price of the share. This is calculated as:

$$\text{NAVPS} = \frac{\text{Assets} - \text{Liabilities}}{\text{Number of shares outstanding}}$$

A mutual fund's assets are held by a custodian. This is usually a bank or trust company that holds onto your money while the manager makes decisions on your behalf. This gives you assurances that the manager will not take off with your money. Other than that, there are no guarantees: mutual funds are subject to the same risks due to price fluctuations as other stocks and bonds.

There are many types of mutual funds available, and this is to your advantage, as you can match the fund's objectives with your own. Do you want income or capital appreciation? Do you want bonds or equities?

Following is an overview of the different types of funds you might invest in:

TYPES OF MUTUAL FUNDS

Equity Funds

Features: Can include blue chip stock as well as more aggressive equities.
Invest In: These funds are placed into common shares.
Main Objective: To create wealth through capital gains accruing over the long term.
Risk Factor: Lower income potential, liquidity.

Global Funds

Features: Seeks the best returns in global markets.
Invest In: Bonds, stocks, equities, money markets.
Main Objective: To turn higher profits through global diversification.
Risk Factor: Volatile international markets, political and economic events, and foreign exchange rates.

Dividend Funds

Features: Seeks the best dividend-producing income return, which has tax advantage if held outside an RRSP.
Invest In: High-quality preferred shares and common shares of taxable Canadian corporations.
Main Objective: To maximize dividend income, achieve capital growth.
Risk Factor: Lower than equities, should be held long term.

Fixed-Income or Bond Funds

Features: Unit prices are stable and income is usually predictable.
Invest In: High-yielding and good-quality government and corporate debt, including high-yielding preferred shares, mortgages and common shares.
Main Objective: Safe principal and high income, long-term capital appreciation.
Risk Factors: Stable, except in periods of interest rate volatility.

Mortgage Funds

Features: Investors hold a piece of several properties, rather than just one.
Invest In: Groups of mortgages, debentures, bonds, short-term securities.
Main Objective: Safe principal and high income.
Risk Factors: Relatively the same as with income funds; affected by interest rate volatility.

Real Estate Funds

Features: Investors can capitalize on future growth of real estate market, and hedge their equity investment against inflation and interest rate fluctuations.
Invest In: All types of real estate.
Main Objective: Reinvestment of income and long-term capital appreciation.
Risk Factors: Liquidity may be low as investor must be in for long term.

Money Markets

Features: Distribution of monthly income.
Invest In: Treasury Bills, commercial paper and short-term government bonds, bankers acceptances.
Main Objectives: High income, liquidity, safe.
Risk Factors: Limited earnings opportunities.

Balanced Funds

Features: A balance of funds is selected according to market conditions and future predictions.
Invest In: Fixed-income securities, common stock, preferred stock.
Main Objective: Mix of income, capital appreciation, safety.
Risk Factors: Dependent on market and economic conditions.

Ethical Funds

Features: Highly selective according to moral viewpoint.
Invest In: Companies that do not profit from certain moral criteria (i.e., armaments).
Main Objective: To make morally correct investment decisions; growth and income.
Risk Factors: Lower liquidity, higher price volatility.

MONEY MANAGEMENT TIP 35

When choosing a mutual fund, it is important to review the fund manager's performance over a period of time. Know the investment objectives of the funds you are previewing and the degree of risk involved, and how long you should expect to hold on to the fund.

Mutual funds have become extremely popular over the past several years and are now sold by banks as well as investment dealers and mutual fund companies. The funds may require minimum investment amounts. Ask your investment dealer about accumulation plans which may allow you to purchase more shares in the fund periodically.

A TYPICAL MUTUAL FUND TABLE
(Source: *The Globe and Mail*)

Fund name	1	2	3	4	5			6				7	8
	Fees	Exp. ratio	RRSP	Vol	3mo	6mo	1yr	2yr	3yr	5yr	10yr	NAVPS	Assets
Name	F1%	1.02%	Y	1	1.26	2.28	3.99	4.43	5.19	7.66	N/A	10.00	37,269

Here is the meaning of the information.

1. **Fees:** N - no sales fees
   F - front-end load
   D - deferred load
   R - redemption fee
2. **Expense Ratio:** Annual ratio of all fees to average net sales
3. **RRSP:** Whether this fund is RRSP eligible
4. **Volatility:** Fluctuation of monthly return over last three years.
   A1 indicates a steady performer; 10 indicates high volatility.
5. **Rate of Return:** 3 mo. 6 mo. 1 yr.
   Per cent changes in value in the period.
6. **Annual Return:** 2 3 5 10 yrs.
   Average annual compound rate of return
7. **NAVPS:** Unit price per share
8. **Assets:** Market value of assets.

Some Drawbacks of Mutual Funds

Mutual funds do have several drawbacks you should enquire about before you invest:
- They are sold as long-term investments and so are not generally meant for investors who wish a quick return in the short term.
- There may be expensive fees attached; watch for "front-end loads" or "back-end loads," which may decrease the longer you keep your money in the fund. Some funds charge only on redemption.
- Watch for expensive "annual fees" on no-load or back-end load funds.

- Ask about management fees and administration costs which can be determined by the fund's expense ratio (total fees as a percentage of average total net assets).
- Management fees are paid regardless of how well—or poorly—your fund performs.

If you are a sophisticated investor, you may wish to compare the price of buying shares directly to the fees charged by the mutual fund. The fees you pay are reflective of the professional management, liquidity and diversification that the funds provide to you. Know about these fees before you invest.

FEE-FOR-SERVICE PLANNERS

Your fee-for-service financial planner can help you meet your investment and retirement goals by charging you an hourly rate for services rendered. You may wish to shop around for a financial planner you feel most comfortable with. Make sure he or she has current income tax knowledge and is experienced with tax-planning matters.

COMMISSION-BASED PLANNERS

Certain firms will take your individual investment requests in exchange for a commission—either from the institution in which the funds are being placed or on each transaction, similar to a stockholder. Look at performance trends carefully and consider diversification if you feel uncomfortable dealing with only one firm.

CHAPTER 23
Real Estate

Unlike many residents of European countries, most Canadians will have the opportunity to own their own homes during their lifetime. Investing in your own home is a major wealth creator, primarily because capital gains accrue tax free. Each family may own one tax-exempt principal residence. Therefore, if you purchased a home in 1990 for $85,000 and find that within five years its market value has increased to $125,000, your $40,000 capital gain (the increase in value over the original cost) can be received on a full tax-free basis.

Capital appreciation on other family residences—such as a cottage, vacation condominium or other revenue property—will be subject to tax in the normal manner (see Part 3).

Real estate is also a good way to earn income; for example, you might rent out your home for a set fee each month to help you pay off your mortgage. As long as capital cost allowance is not claimed on the home, your tax-exempt status is maintained.

You might also own rental properties in addition to your principal residence. These investments can bring income (rents) and capital appreciation. In general, they are considered long-term investments that are subject to market fluctuations. Local market conditions and interest rates have a profound effect on the quality of real estate investments. Only net rental income (gross rents less allowable expenses) is reported on the tax return. Net losses on rental operations can be used to offset other income of the year provided a profit motive can be established. Rental losses cannot be increased or created with capital cost allowance claims.

TYPES OF REAL ESTATE INVESTMENTS

1. Your principal residence: a house, condominium, mobile home, etc.
2. Vacation properties.
3. Vacant land.
4. Residential properties: boarding houses, apartments.

5. Commercial properties: office buildings, shopping centres, industrial centres.
6. Farming property.

In making the decision to acquire real property, one hard question that must be asked is this: *Will the cost of borrowing money to buy the property be less than what I can earn from it over the long term?*

If the answer will be "yes," you probably have a good investment on your hands.

Variable Cost Factors to Consider

- Interest rates.
- Property taxes.
- Repairs and maintenance.
- Insurance costs.

What will the return on your investment be once you have factored in all of your costs? This can be computed using the following formula:

$$\text{Rate of return} = \frac{\text{Net income before depreciation}}{\text{Acquisition cost}}$$

Therefore, if the property cost you $140,000, and your net income for the year is $5,000, your rate of return is only 3.4 per cent. If you take out your interest costs of, let's say, $10,000, the return on your investment is almost 11 per cent.

Compare this to the annual appreciation—or depreciation—of the value of the property. Like most of your other investments, you must consider why you are holding the real estate; you need to see a reasonable return on your investment over a period of time. If your net rate of return after operating costs is only 3.4 per cent, calculate what rate of capital appreciation is required to bring you the total return you require.

Remember the "Rule of 72": At a rate of return of only 3.4 per cent, it will take 21 years for you to double your money (72 divided by 3.4 per cent).

Advantages of Holding Real Estate

1. A hedge against inflation: investment of today's dollars to earn future capital appreciation that should out-pace the inflation rate.
2. An ongoing income producer to offset rental costs.
3. Tax advantages: exempt principal residence status, rental losses, capital gains treatment.

Disadvantages of Holding Real Estate

1. Liquidity: How fast can you sell if you have to?
2. Initial Investment: Do you have the down payment you need to make the acquisition?
3. Cyclical Market: Can you ride out the price volatility in the real estate marketplace?
4. Interest Rate Volatility: Can you afford the risk of higher interest rates at mortgage renewal?
5. Unpredictable Income: How long can you afford not to have tenants in the building?

Options for Holding Real Estate

1. Sole ownership.
2. Joint ownership.
3. Unit holder of a limited partnership.
4. Mutual funds.

Recent history has shown us that real estate was a very good investment during inflationary times. However, when the recession hit, there was a general downturn in real estate prices in many local markets. Many people lost their investments outright.

> **MONEY MANAGEMENT TIP 36**
>
> In buying real estate, timing and liquidity are critical. Take this into account before you commit yourself.

CHAPTER 24
Your Portfolio Mix

Every small business has a two-fold goal in its operations: ongoing income production and the growth of the original capital investment of its owner(s). A business owner uses capital—cash, machinery, land, buildings, inventory—to earn income and increase equity over time. Equity is "net worth"—the difference between the assets and the liabilities of the firm.

You might think of your "investment portfolio" in much the same way. Your goal is to increase the value of your financial assets—your cash, the securities you own, the residences you own, etc.—while earning ongoing income from your investments. If you were to assign a specific task or "job" to your capital or "working dollars," you might classify them into categories, as for example:

Job Description for My Invested Capital

1. To generate income.
2. To grow in accrued value in order to generate future capital gains.
3. To minimize or balance out any declines in the dollar value.
4. To maintain purchasing power over a period of time.
5. To avoid loss of original capital investment, if possible.

How important each of these tasks is to you will largely depend upon your age, your risk tolerance level and your asset mix. For example, seniors must count on the income generated by their invested capital to offset expenses. They may be very concerned about generating "income" from their investments as well as the growth of their capital. But how do they deal with the recent low interest rates that have cut some seniors' living standards in half?

Younger people, on the other hand, usually have income from other sources to pay for current expenses. Their investments serve primarily a different purpose—to cause the capital to grow. But what if they lose their jobs or businesses?

All investors must be very conscious of the future purchasing power of their money (inflationary trends must be monitored) and the possibility that their capital might diminish (recessionary/deflationary trends). The performance of invested principal to produce income when needed is also important.

You may wish to make up a "Priorities Chart" now, similar to the one below, to classify what tasks you expect of your investment dollars. This is a process you may wish to undertake with your money manager, financial planner and/or tax advisor.

YOUR INVESTMENT PRIORITIES
Choose your age level and indicate your priorities.

Objective	Age	Very Important	Important	Minor Importance
Income from Investments	18-44			✔
	45-65		✔	
	over 65	✔		
Growth of Capital	18-44	✔		
	45-65	✔		
	over 65			✔
Preservation of Capital	18-44		✔	
	45-65		✔	
	over 65	✔		
Preservation of Purchasing Power	18-44	✔		
	45-65	✔		
	over 65	✔		

Once you have determined which factors are most important to you at your current age, you can begin to develop plans for the types of investments you should have in your investment portfolio.

A general rule of thumb has been to program in riskier, longer-term investments for younger investors. You may have heard the simplistic guideline: "Take your age, subtract it from 100, and that is the percentage of your portfolio that should be exposed to risk."

Following this advice would mean that a 60-year-old should have no more than 40 per cent of their portfolio in unsecured investments, while a 28-year-old could look at up to 72 per cent in equities or other riskier longer-term investments.

The reality is that many of the decisions surrounding where to place your capital will be determined by the following:

PRIMARY DETERMINANTS FOR ASSET SELECTION

- The amount of capital you have.
- Your age.
- How many dependants you have.

- Your risk tolerance level.
- The performance of your asset mix.
- Tax considerations.
- Economic conditions and trends.

The ideal is to maximize after-tax returns and minimize risk. This is where your professional money manager and tax advisor can perform wonders for you. The money manager's role is to select the appropriate asset mix according to the amount of money you have, and your risk-tolerance level. If he or she is good at what they do, they will ensure you get the highest returns for the lowest amount of risk, by shrewdly diversifying your investments.

For example: Thomas and Susan each have $100,000 to invest.

Thomas's Investment Manager Chooses

$ 50,000	in T-Bills	@	18.0%	return
30,000	in Bonds	@	12.0%	return
20,000	in Stocks	@	14.0%	return
$100,000			10.4%	return

Susan's Investment Manager Chooses

$ 20,000	in T-Bills	@	7.5%	return
50,000	in Bonds	@	11.0%	return
30,000	in Stocks	@	13.5%	return
$100,000			11.0%	return

Source: The Equion Group/Loring Ward Investment Counsel Ltd.

What this illustration shows is that while Susan's investments had an overall lower return than Thomas's, her overall portfolio reaped a higher return simply because of the asset allocation mix.

No portfolio selection would be complete without a view of the tax considerations. The first question that must be answered is whether or not the client is maximizing RRSP contribution room. Investments held "inside" a tax-sheltered RRSP account will likely have a different asset mix from those held "outside" the RRSP in a tax-exposed account (see Part 3 for "The Tax Slant"). This is because you want the earnings that attract the highest tax liability to be tax sheltered in the RRSP.

Once your investment priorities and determinants for asset selection are identified, you can match investments to your needs. For example:

SAMPLE MENU OF INVESTMENT OPTIONS
$100,000 Portfolio

Job Description for Your Assets	Type of Investment	Emphasis/Goals	Asset Allocation Mix*
Liquid Assets or Cash Equivalents	Treasury Bills, commercial paper, provincial government bonds.	Lower yields; but instant availability.	
Income from Investments (Conservative)	Dividend-producing preferred or common stocks, debentures, GICs, T-Bills, government guaranteed bonds.	Watch current yields and anticipate future yields.	
Growth of Capital	Common stocks, real estate, certain mutual funds, convertible debentures, some senior capitalized companies (i.e., banks, utilities), and some smaller-growth companies.	Long-term capital gains; little investment income.	
Preservation of Capital	Certain mutual funds, real estate, preferred stocks, highly rated corporate bonds, government guaranteed bonds, P1 rated preferred shares.	Dollar values should not drop; potential for appreciation.	
Protection of Future Purchasing Power	Real estate, certain mutual funds. Common and preferred stocks, real return bonds, short-term government bonds, short-term GICs.	A hedge against inflation. Capital appreciation must outperform inflation rate.	

*Ask your financial advisor to help you fill in the correct mix, depending on your age, amount of investment in the portfolio, and risk tolerance.

As you can tell, together with your investment advisor, you can best determine how to "balance" your investment selection with your income and capital growth needs.

We have spoken earlier about your risk tolerance level. Gord Wimble, Branch Manager and Vice-President of Wood Gundy, Winnipeg, recommends you focus on two types of risk.

1. *Credit Risk*: Will the issuer of a bond be able to stay in business and repay your principal plus interest?

2. *Market Risk*: Will your investment decline in value because of market forces (i.e., bond prices fall when interest rates go up). While most investments you buy through a stockbroker can be converted quickly to cash by selling them on the open market, you could be forced to do so at a loss.

Your investment advisor must focus on your investment objectives of the day in helping you to select the proper investments. If you have some tolerance for the risk of loss, your advisor can select equities or mutual funds to provide some growth. However, if you must live on the earnings generated by your investments, there is no room to risk any of your principal, and your focus must be on achieving a real after-tax and after-inflation return.

In making your plans, don't forget to consider what will happen once you want to receive your money back out of the investments you have chosen. Will you be able to get back what you've put into them? Where will you invest your money next?

These questions explore the difference between "marketability"—your ability to find another buyer to take your investments off your hands—and "liquidity"—turning your investment back into the cash you paid for it.

Be forewarned. There is no "right" or "wrong" portfolio mix. In fact, you may wish to consult with two or three investment advisors to get their opinions on the correct "mix" for your goals and objectives at the current time. You may find that each will have a different viewpoint.

As well, changing market and economic forces will ensure that no investment strategy is ever etched in stone. Most investment counsellors will admit it is a bit of a moving target, to say the least. A good eye on economic cycles and global trends is required.

And remember, often what you gain on a guaranteed investment security (little risk), you will lose to taxes, inflation and lost growth potential. Keep an open mind to some risk accumulation that is offset to higher after-tax yields.

DIVERSIFICATION: IDEAS FOR ACHIEVING BALANCE
IN YOUR INVESTMENT PORTFOLIO

Investment Type	Reason	% Invested at Age:		
		25-44	45-65	Over 65
1. *Liquid Assets:* Bank account, Short-term notes, T-Bills	-Emergencies -Opportunity for investments -Liquidity	5-10%	5-10%	5-10%
2. *Conservative Investments:* Fixed income securities such as GICs, bonds, debentures, preferred shares, certain mutual funds,	-Income -Protection -Safety -Yield -Liquidity	10-50%	50-75%	75-100%
3. *Moderate Level of Risk:* Mutual funds, stocks, convertible debentures	-Growth -Income	25-75%	45-65%	0-25%
4. *Riskier Investments:* Commodities, real estate, business interests, mutual funds, stocks	-Diversification -Growth -Income	0-25%	0-25%	0-25%
5. *Very Risky Investments:* Precious metals, art, certain new offerings and securities, certain real estate	-Diversification -Growth	0-25%	0-25%	0-25%

MONEY MANAGEMENT TIP 37

The goal of diversification is to spread out or minimize risk while maximizing the return on your investments now and in the future. Discuss your options with your investment dealer.

As market conditions change, your asset mix should be reviewed. Some financial advisors like to do such a portfolio review twice a year; others quarterly. At the very least, you should take a close look at your monthly financial statements and monitor the progress in your account. You may find your objectives and your risk tolerance level are also evolving. Speak to your financial professional about the new opportunities for income and growth available to you in the financial marketplace.

CHAPTER 25
Protecting Your Purchasing Power

Even if you do everything right and accumulate your targeted nest egg, a few obstacles will come your way, unfortunately, to put a dent into our basic theories of yield maximization and capital appreciation. One of them is inflation. Another is your tax liability, which will be discussed in Part 3.

Someone once said that inflation rewards those who owe money, and harms those who save it.

Inflation dilutes the purchasing power of your savings in the future. In an inflationary period, persons who have a high concentration of Guaranteed Investment Certificates, Canada Savings Bonds or other "safe" investments are particularly at risk.

This is because the present value of their savings will erode in the future. In dealing with inflation, you must be prepared to pay more in the future for all of your needs.

For example, how much will $1.00 of savings today be worth when you retire if the following inflation rates persisted? How does this affect a capital accumulation of half a million dollars?

FUTURE VALUE OF $1.00 TODAY

Inflation Rate	Years from Now	Future Value	x Savings ($500,000) = Purchasing Power
2%	10	.82	$410,174
	20	.67	$336,486
	30	.55	$276,035
	40	.45	$226,445

Inflation Rate	Years from Now	Future Value	x Savings ($500,000) = Purchasing Power
7%	10	.51	$254,175
	20	.26	$129,210
	30	.13	$ 65,684
	40	.07	$ 33,390

YIKES!

What this means is that even at a low inflation rate of 2 per cent, you must plan for the fact that inflation will erode your purchasing power in the future.

How do you do this? Diversification, of course. During inflationary times, your real return on interest-bearing investments falls dramatically. If that's where all your invested capital lies, you'll be losing, not gaining ground. When you add in the effects of high personal taxation, your real return may, in fact, be very low. Some experts believe that real estate is the key investment during inflationary times. (Gains are tax deferred, interest is tax deductible and capital appreciation is often high.) If you can manage to sell your property at the end of an inflationary ride, you'll stand to profit handsomely.

However, what happens to these investments if you missed your opportunity to sell, and find yourself smack in the middle of a recession, or possibly a depression?

In recessionary times, prices fall and, as we have seen globally in the early 1990s, the values of real estate, businesses, common stocks and other equities fall or collapse. As a result, the income from your investments—wages, rental income, business income and dividend income—also fall, or you can lose outright.

Therefore, *your goal in a recessionary period is to preserve the value of your assets so that you can maintain your income levels*. You and your financial advisor may be looking for safe and secure investments now, such as bonds or GICs, because despite lower interest rates than those during inflationary periods, your purchasing power has actually increased.

MONEY MANAGEMENT TIP 38

Understand the consequences of inflation and deflation and match your investment strategy accordingly.

However, if you expect an economic upswing over the next several years, including higher interest rates, your fixed-income securities may be best held in shorter terms to maximize opportunities to invest at higher interest rates one, two or three years from now.

For the keen investor, maximizing all investment opportunities thus becomes a fine art that evolves with economic cycles and changing personal objectives.

THE TAX SLANT

CHAPTER 26
The Warm-up Routine

No personal money management plan would be complete without a solid grounding in how income is taxed in Canada and what provisions are available to taxpayers to minimize that tax. Tax planning is a major component of your personal financial plan and should never be minimized or ignored either because of its apparent complexity or the fact that most Canadians equate tax planning to the calculation of their annual income tax return.

> **MONEY MANAGEMENT TIP 39**
>
> Prepare your tax return each and every year on time. Do your tax planning all year long.

Few taxpayers realize just how significant their contribution to the tax rolls of the country really is. If you take the example of an average Canadian who earns $30,000 annually over a working life of approximately 40 years, his gross earning potential is $1.2 million. At an average combined federal/provincial tax rate of 27 per cent, this taxpayer can expect to pay $324,000 in income taxes alone during his lifetime.

Your income tax liability is akin to paying off a mortgage. It's the price we pay for living in the best country in the world. The income taxes you pay can be legally and legitimately reduced, using the provisions available to us under the Income Tax Act. If someone told you of several ways to reduce your mortgage by thousands of dollars, wouldn't you be interested? Likewise, a knowledge of personal tax rules may just shave thousands of dollars off your overall tax bill.

Tax planning, then, can be defined as the arranging of your affairs, within the framework of the law, so as to pay the least amount of taxes possible and keep the highest after-tax return.

Tax planning begins with a close look at your tax returns since 1985. This is the farthest year a taxpayer can go back to for recovery of missed tax provisions. Many taxpayers find themselves in receipt of thousands of dollars of overpaid taxes due to missed provisions when such a "prior year tax review" is taken.

> **MONEY MANAGEMENT TIP 40**
>
> Review your prior filed tax returns to recover missed tax deductions or credits.

Watch for commonly missed items such as the Federal Sales Tax Credit (1986 to 1990), the Disability Credit (for severe and prolonged disabilities), carrying charges (such as your safety deposit box and investment counsel fees), missed medical expenses (such as your Blue Cross or other private health insurance payments), the $1,000 interest and dividend deduction (1985 to 1987), and transfers of tuition and education credits from child to parent or between spouses.

To recover missed provisions, write a letter to Revenue Canada requesting the adjustment on their form T1ADJ. Attach all supporting documentation.

The next step is to extract certain key figures from your prior filed returns.

CARRYOVER PROVISIONS ON YOUR TAX RETURNS

1. Unused office in the home expenses since 1988.
2. Unused non-capital losses of prior years.
3. Unused net capital losses of prior years.
4. Capital gains deductions previously used.
5. Cumulative Net Investment Loss balances.
6. RRSP contribution room.
7. Previously reported interest on compounding GICs and bonds.
8. Unused charitable donations of the prior five years.
9. Unused medical expenses of the immediately preceding year.
10. Unused moving expenses of the immediately preceding year.
11. Paid but unclaimed maintenance payments for up to one year before a written agreement or court order.
12. Unused Business Investment Losses.
13. Any Undepreciated Capital Cost Balances.

Bringing forward these numbers every year will reduce the taxes you pay and create new disposable income sources for you. For example:

1. *Unused office in the home expenses.* If you are a commission salesperson or run a small business from your home, you may have had your claim for office in the home restricted due to prior year losses. However, now you are making lots of money and need every write-off you can get! Bring forward those unused office in the home expenses and apply them against your business income this year.

2. *Unused non-capital losses of prior years.* These are losses from activities such as employment, revenue properties and small businesses that exceeded income in prior years. Such losses are most valuable to you now, as you can use these amounts to reduce other income of the year. Non-capital losses can either be carried back three years or carried forward seven years before they expire.

3. *Unused capital losses of prior years.* These losses arise from the disposition of an asset at less than its adjusted cost base. Adjusted cost base is what you paid for the asset plus any additions or improvements. It can also be its fair market value if it was transferred to you or held during a specific valuation date. Capital losses can only be applied against other capital gains of the year, but can be carried forward indefinitely or back and applied against capital gains in the previous three years. In the year of death, they can be used to offset other taxable income in full. This is a little-known fact that can save the beneficiaries thousands of dollars.

4. *Capital Gains Deductions previously used.* Even though the $100,000 Capital Gains Deduction was eliminated in the February 22, 1994 federal budget, 1994 is the final year for which accrued gains on investments will qualify for this deduction. The government will allow a one-time election to report such accrued gains on the 1994 tax return, for the purposes of using up the deduction. The deduction claimable is reduced by any capital gains deduction previously used, so carry-forward information is very important to avoid overstatement of the available amounts. As the $500,000 Super Exemption for qualified small business corporations and qualified farms is still with us, capital gains deduction balances will still require tracking into the future.

5. *Cumulative Net Investment Losses (CNIL).* The excess of investment expenses claimed since 1988 over investment income reported in the

same period is the CNIL balance. The government will not allow both the net investment expense write-offs and the capital gains deduction. Therefore, your CNIL balance, if any, will reduce your capital gains deduction.

6. *RRSP Contribution Room.* This figure tells you how much "room" you have to make contributions to your RRSP. It is made up of "room" available since 1991. The "room" refers to the difference between what you could have contributed to an RRSP and what you did contribute. Therefore, if your cumulative room in the period 1991 to 1993 was $25,000 and you contributed $15,000 in that time, your available "room" is $10,000.

7. *Interest previously reported on compounding investments.* In Canada, since 1990, we must report interest accruing on compounding investments every year. Compounding investments acquired before 1990 must be reported at least every three years. Therefore, it is most important to bring forward the information about previously reported amounts so that you don't double report interest in the year of maturity or redemption.

8. *Unused charitable donations.* In 1994 and future years, our tax system allows us to claim 17 per cent of the first $200 in charitable donations we make in the year and 29 per cent of the balance. Therefore, if your donations are under $200, it may pay you to take advantage of a tax loophole that allows you to "save" your charity expenses for up to five years to maximize the use of the 29 per cent credit.

9. *Unused medical expenses.* Medical expense claims must be reduced by 3 per cent of your net income and consequently often do not qualify for a credit. However, you can save your medical expenses to encompass a 12-month period ending in the tax year. Therefore, save your receipts over two or three tax years to maximize this claim. Also consider transferring these expenses to your spouse, if their income is lower.

10. *Unclaimed moving expenses.* Taxpayers who move at least 40 kilometres closer to a new work or business location may claim moving expenses against income earned at the new location. If there was no income earned, the amounts can be carried forward to the next tax year to offset income earned. This tax deduction can amount to lucrative five-figure claims. Don't miss out.

11. *Unclaimed maintenance payments.* Under rules in effect at the time of writing, a payer of alimony or maintenance could deduct these amounts in the year of separation (as per a court order or written agreement) and up to one year previous. Therefore, keep all records of payments made as soon as your conjugal relationship breaks down.

12. *Unclaimed Business Investment Losses (BILs).* The recession of the late 1980s claimed many small business corporations. If shares or debt owed to you became uncollectible, you may have incurred an allowable business investment loss, three-quarters of which can be used to reduce other income of the year. Excess or unused portions of such losses can be carried back three years (as non-capital losses) and forward seven years to reduce other income in those years. After the seven-year period, they become capital losses that can be carried forward indefinitely and applied against capital gains of the year. Therefore, track such losses carefully.

13. *Undepreciated Capital Cost Balances.* The undepreciated value of your income producing assets, used in business or, in some cases, employment, can create a lucrative tax deduction for you, at your option. Speak to your tax advisor about your capital cost allowance claims.

> **MONEY MANAGEMENT TIP 41**
>
> Take the time to track unused carryover provisions from prior tax years. Like the incredible power of compounding on savings of a dollar a day, alert taxpayers can save thousands of dollars by paying attention to their taxpayer rights.

CHAPTER 27
How Income Is Taxed in Canada

Taxable income sources you may earn fall into several tax categories which are summarized below:

TAX OBLIGATIONS ON INCOME SOURCES

Some Exempt Income Sources
- refundable tax credits
- gifts or inheritances
- Goods and Services Tax Credit prepayments
- Child Tax Benefits
- income earned by Status Indians on reserves
- life insurance policy proceeds on death of the insured
- personal injury awards
- private health insurance payments (not funded by employer)
- profit from the sale of principal residence

Fully Taxable
- employment income
- commission income
- unemployment insurance benefits
- pension income
- interest income
- net rental income
- net business income
- alimony/maintenance*

*Subject to outcome of appeal of Thibideau case in which it was ruled that such payments should not be taxable to the recipient.

Special Tax Provisions
- dividends
- certain foreign pensions
- scholarships/bursaries

PART 3 The Tax Slant 95

Asset Appreciation
- capital gains provisions

Exempt Income Sources Such receipts need not be reported on the tax return at all.

Fully Taxable Sources These receipts must be reported in full (100 per cent) as income on the tax return.

Special Tax Provisions Dividends are treated differently for tax purposes because they represent the after-tax distribution of profits of a company. The actual dividends received are increased or "grossed up" by 25 per cent. Then an offsetting "dividend tax credit" of 13.33 per cent of the grossed-up amount is used as a dollar-for-dollar reduction of federal taxes payable. The result of this calculation is a lower marginal tax rate on dividends as opposed to interest income.

In the case of foreign pensions, certain countries with whom Canada has tax treaties exempt portions of certain Canadian income sources paid to non-residents, and vice versa. For example, Canadian residents in receipt of U.S. Social Security may claim a deduction for 50 per cent of such income received, for 1994 and prior tax years. Certain German pensions received are exempt from tax altogether.

Students in receipt of scholarships or bursaries can claim an exemption on the first $500 of the award. The balance is taxable in full.

Asset Appreciation Special rules exist for situations where a gain or loss is incurred on the disposition of a capital asset. The key word here is "disposition." No tax consequence will arise on accrued gains on your assets until a disposition takes place. (Exception: In 1994 we have a one time opportunity to pre-report such accrued gains for the purposes of using up available capital gains deductions.)

WHEN A CAPITAL DISPOSITION OCCURS
- When an asset is sold.
- When an asset is converted from business to personal use.
- When an asset is gifted or transferred to someone.
- Upon emigration from Canada.
- Upon conversion, redemption or cancellation of a share.
- When an option to acquire or dispose of shares expires.
- When property is transferred to a trust.
- When property is transferred into an RRSP.
- When a debt owed is settled or cancelled.
- When the taxpayer dies.

When you are in receipt of the various income sources identified above, you will add them to income (except for exempt sources) and calculate the tax you must pay on the total. The tax you actually pay, divided by your taxable income, is called your "effective tax rate."

> **MONEY MANAGEMENT TIP 42**
>
> Learn to understand how various income sources are taxed in Canada in order to diversify investments with a tax-planning viewpoint.

To find out how much tax you'll pay on the next dollar you earn, you need to know what your marginal tax rate is. This is particularly significant in judging the after-tax yields on your investments.

CHAPTER 28
Canada's Tax Rates

In Canada, the federal government levies personal income taxes and collects personal income taxes for each of the provinces except Quebec. We must file one tax return to accomplish this task, except in Quebec, where both a federal and provincial income tax return must be filed.

The federal tax rates (the same for all Canadians) are the following:

FEDERAL PERSONAL INCOME TAX RATES
as at time of writing for tax years 1992 to 1994

Taxable Income	Rate
On the first $29,589	17%
$29,590 to $59,180	26%
over $59,180	29%

In addition, provincial tax rates, which vary from province to province, must be added to the federal rate for a complete snapshot of taxes payable. They are expressed as a percentage of "Basic Federal Tax" and can include a variety of surtaxes and credit systems. On average, federal/provincial tax rates can be estimated as follows:

AVERAGE FEDERAL/PROVINCIAL MARGINAL TAX RATES
as at the time of writing for tax years 1992 to 1994

Taxable Income	Rate		
	Fully Taxable Salary/Pensions/Interest	Dividends	Capital Gains
On the first $29,589	27%	8%	21%
$29,590 to $59,180	42%	26%	31%
over $59,180	49%	33%	36%

The rates quoted above represent "marginal" rates of tax; that is, how much tax will you pay on the next dollar of income you earn?

You will notice a couple of things immediately upon looking at this chart:

Dividends vs. Interest. At the lowest tax bracket, you'll reap 19 per cent in tax savings by earning dividends rather than interest; 16 per cent more at the middle bracket and 16 per cent again in the top tax bracket.

Capital Gains vs. Interest. Your tax savings are 6 per cent at the lowest tax bracket, 11 per cent less is paid in the mid-tax bracket, and 13 per cent less at the top tax bracket. (We have assumed no capital gains deduction is available.)

Therefore, those investors who have all their eggs in fixed-income securities are feeling the taxman's pinch more dramatically than those whose diversified earnings result in a combination of interest, dividends or capital gains.

To refresh your memory, remember that interest results from investments in debt instruments such as GICs, Canada Savings Bonds, provincial or municipal government bonds, Treasury Bills and so on.

Dividends are earned when a company in which you are the owner or part-owner by virtue of share acquisition, declares a distribution of after-tax profits to its shareholders. The actual dividends you receive are shown on a T5 Slip. This figure is not reported on the tax return. Rather, you must report a "grossed up" amount—the actual dividend times 1.25—as the "taxable dividend." This is shown in the T5 Slip and recorded on the T1 General and the tax return. Finally, the T5 Slip will indicate the Dividend Tax Credit, which is calculated as 13.33 per cent of the taxable dividend. This figure is recorded on Schedule 1 and is used to reduce the federal taxes you must pay.

A *capital gain* will occur when you dispose of an income-producing asset such as a share in a company. The marginal tax rates shown above assume that the capital gain is calculated at today's income inclusion rate of 75 per cent.

Example:
Tom buys 100 shares of XYZ Company in Year 1 for $1,000. He sells them in Year 2 for $1,300. He reports on his tax return, Schedule 3, his capital gain of $300. He reports as taxable income, on page 1 of the T1 General, the "taxable portion" of this gain: 75 per cent of $300 or $225.

> **MONEY MANAGEMENT TIP 43**
> Know and understand the various tax rates applied to your income in Canada.

CHAPTER 29
What a Difference a Move Can Make!

From a personal tax point of view, what is the most expensive province to live in? What is the least expensive province? The spreads are truly remarkable, and can have a significant bearing on how much money stays in your jeans at the end of the year!

An understanding of provincial tax rates will help you decide when to make an interprovincial move. Timing must be planned to take advantage of the lowest possible tax rates, and to maximize the claim you can make under the "moving expenses" deduction on Line 219 of the T1 General.

Itemized below are estimated average federal/provincial tax rates. These are subject to change annually with both federal and provincial budgets. It is, therefore, important to keep abreast of the actual tax effects of your move before you go. It would be a good idea to have a tax professional do a preliminary tax calculation for you before you pack up and go.

AVERAGE FEDERAL/PROVINCIAL TAX RATES
as at time of writing for 1992 to 1994

Bracket*: Province	Salary 1	Pension 2	Interest 3	Dividends 1	Dividends 2	Dividends 3	Capital Gains 1	Capital Gains 2	Capital Gains 3
BC	25%	42%	50%	7%	25%	34%	20%	31%	37%
AB	25	39	45	7	24	30	19	29	34
SK	28	43	51	10	28	36	22	33	38
MB	28	44	50	10	30	36	21	33	37
ON	27	43	51	7	26	34	21	31	38
NB	27	43	49	8	26	33	21	32	37
NS	27	42	49	8	26	33	21	32	36
PEI	27	41	49	8	26	33	21	32	36
NF	28	45	51	8	27	34	22	34	38
YK	25	39	45	7	24	30	19	30	34
NWT	25	39	44	7	23	30	19	29	33
Average	27	42	49	8	26	33	21	31	36

*Bracket: 1 = less than $29,590
2 = $29,590 to $59,180
3 = over $59,180

At the time of writing, Alberta stood out as the province with the overall lowest personal income taxes in almost every tax bracket and for almost every income source.

The other provinces varied, taxing some income sources higher than others. B.C. has a good overall tax treatment of all income sources; Ontario's tax rates have crept up on high-income earners particularly.

With an understanding of how your income is taxed in the different provinces, you can now plan to time your move so that it is at your tax advantage, and not the government's.

Here's the trick. In Canada our income for the entire year is taxed at our province of residence as at December 31 of the tax year. This means that if you moved to Alberta on December 1, your income for the entire year would be taxed at the lower Alberta provincial tax rates. You'd be receiving a bonus by way of your income tax refund.

However, if you weren't paying attention, and moved from Alberta to Ontario before year end, your taxes would go up 6 points—for income over $59,180—if you were earning pensions/salary or interest. Ouch!

If you have no choice and must move to take an employment position before year-end, try to negotiate a tax "cushion" from your employer if you end up on the wrong side of the tax fence.

Then, don't forget to claim your moving expenses. Many Canadians are not aware of the lucrative tax deduction that can be claimed to compensate you for your unreimbursed moving expenses. Pensioners moving to B.C. watch out—the move must be made to earn a salary, wages or for self-employment income. For students, scholarships/bursaries must be received. If your only income is from "passive sources" such as pensions, investments or even unemployment insurance, you'll be out of luck. However, a one year carry-forward of expenses is allowed should you have the required earned income then.

If you qualify to make the claim, you'll be able to write off the costs of selling your home in the old location, including real estate commissions, penalties for paying off the mortgage before maturity, and legal and advertising costs. You'll be able to write off the costs of transfer or "welcome taxes" at the new location, as well as legal fees.

Enroute, you'll be able to claim removal expenses, including costs of the mover, insurance for household effects and costs of moving your boat, trailer or mobile home. Keep all bills for your auto expenses, including gas and oil and food expenditures while you are on the road. These will be claimable on your tax return.

MONEY MANAGEMENT TIP 44

Before you move within Canada, know the tax consequences. It is an investment in time and effort that could save you thousands of dollars.

CHAPTER 30
The Basics of Tax Planning

When Canadians think about taxes, they usually think about filing their income tax returns. This activity, largely completed in the period March 1 to April 30 every year, is a reconciliation of the past year's income, deductions and credits. It's history. With the exception of buying an RRSP within the first 60 days of the new year, there is little influence you can have on your tax affairs next spring, except to prepare your return with a keen eye for every tax provision you are entitled to. (For a detailed step-by-step, line-by-line instructional guide on preparing your personal income tax return, be sure to pick up a copy of *Jacks on Tax Savings*.)

> **MONEY MANAGEMENT TIP 45**
>
> Almost every event—personal and financial—that happens to you throughout the year has some kind of a tax consequence. Be sure to diarize lifetime events for use during tax time.

TAX TIME EVENTS DIARY

Your Events Diary might include the following, for example:

Lifetime Event | **Tax Consequence**

1. A New Conjugal Relationship
- If common law, claim as single until one year has passed; after one year you are considered "married" for tax purposes. With child(ren), see #2 below.
- Possible claim for the Spousal Amount.
- Possibility of transferring education/tuition credits to spouse.
- Possible transfer of medical expenses/charities/political contributions to spouse for more advantageous results.
- Possibility of transferring pension credit to spouse.
- Possibility of transferring disability amount to spouse.
- Contribution to a spousal RRSP.
- Changes to provincial tax credits.
- Income-splitting possibilities.

Lifetime Event	Tax Consequence
2. Birth of a Child	• Apply for the Child Tax Benefit payment. • Start a tax-free education fund by depositing the CTB in a separate account for that child. • Income sources change: UIC maternity benefits are subject to tax and do not qualify for RRSP earned-income purposes. • Possible claim for Spousal Amount by the other parent. • Possible claim for Equivalent-to-Spouse amount for single parents. • Possible child support payments. • New deduction for child care expenses.
3. Post-Secondary Education	• Receipt of scholarships, bursaries or research grants qualify for special tax treatment. • Possibility of claiming moving expenses. • Claim for education/tuition amount by student. • Transfer of unused education/tuition amount to supporting individual including spouse, parent or grandparent. • Special claims under the child care provisions. • File own return to recover GST Prepayment credits. • Possible CPP premium overpayments if under 18 during the year.
4. A New Job	• Immediate RRSP savings should begin. • Possible new deductions for union dues/company pension. • Negotiation for tax-free or taxable benefits. • Unreimbursed expenses for auto, supplies, home office should be tracked for tax deductibility. Form T2200 must be signed by employer. • Purchase of Canada Savings Bonds on payroll plan —don't forget to claim the carrying charges. • Moving expense claims. • Employee home relocation loan deduction. • Stock options and shares deductions. • Northern Residents Deduction for qualifying areas. • First-time GST-370 Rebate claims. • Possible board and lodging claims for long-distance transport employees.

Lifetime Event	Tax Consequence
5. A New Business	• Proprietorship or incorporation? • Choose fiscal year-end to your best tax advantage. • Time asset acquisitions for maximum tax advantage. • Split income to family members. • Use RRSP room to maximum advantage. • Set up home office. • Maintain automobile driving log. • Audit-proof your claims with documentation. • Attend two tax-deductible conventions each year.
6. New Investments	• If RRSP eligible and taxable, consider RRSP contribution first. • Consider after-tax return on your investments earned outside an RRSP. • If you borrow to invest, deduct interest charges. Deduct your safety deposit box costs. • Track all interest pre-reported on compounding investments. • Pre-report accrued interest annually (pre-1990 compounding investments must be reported at least every three years). • Have lower-income earner invest money so that returns are taxed at lower margin tax rates. • Track CNIL and any Minimum Taxes paid. • Time capital dispositions to your maximum advantage. • Use loss carryovers to your maximum advantage. • Split investment income with family members. (However, beware of attribution rules.)
7. Retirement	• Plan for RRSP rollover of eligible retiring allowances. • Plan to rollover up to $6,000 of pension income to spouse's RRSP (this provision ends with 1994 tax filing year). • Lower income in retirement may open eligibility for GST credits or provincial tax credits. • Transfer dividends to higher-income earner if • Spousal Amount is thereby increased or created. • Maximize RRSP contribution based on unused room of prior years. • Plan to make quarterly instalment payments, if necessary.

Lifetime Event	Tax Consequence
	• Consider when to convert RRSP savings to annuity and/or RRIF based on income requirements.
• Split CPP benefits receivable with spouse if advantageous.
• Plan for Old Age Security clawbacks.
• Plan for clawback of Age Amount.
• Split investment income with family members (beware of attribution rules).
• Consider part-time employment/business to create new RRSP room.
• Revisit emergency fund needs (liquidity of investments).
• Medical expense and charitable donation claims could change in light of advancing age. Revisit rules, and consider which spouse gets maximum benefit from claims.
• Possible CPP premium overpayment.
• Transfer age, liability, pension, education or tuition amounts to spouse.
8. Death	• Deemed disposition of all assets at fair market value at date of death.
• Rollover of RRSPs to spouse or dependent children.
• Utilization of unused capital and non-capital losses.
• Carry back of excess medical expenses/charitable donations.
• No GST Credit claimable—survivor must receive.
• Make RRSP contribution to spousal plan to reduce income.
• Possible Spousal Claim to surviving spouse.
• Transfer pension income amount, tuition/education, pension or disability amount to surviving spouse.
• Possible transfer of dividends to surviving spouse if Spousal Amount is created or increased.
• Prorate investment and pension income to date of death.
• Surviving spouse must report CPP death benefits.
• Other death benefits may qualify for $10,000 exemption.
• Optional returns may be filed for right or things (amounts not paid at death such as salary or vacation

Lifetime Event	Tax Consequence
	pay for period ending before death, uncashed but matured bond coupons, bond interest earned but not paid or previously reported, businesses or partnerships. • Income earned by trust set up after death may yield income. • Reinvestment of life insurance policy proceeds. • Utilization of any previously paid Minimum Tax carryovers.
9. New Residences	• Calculate cost of land and building. • Keep track of all additions and improvements. • Report any rental income. • Partition off any office in home space. • Keep track of any business appointments or, in case of babysitting enterprises, hours of operation. • Keep track of utility costs, maintenance and repairs, and insurance if you run a business out of your home.
10. Extended U.S. Vacations	• Are you a "resident alien" required to file a U.S. return on all worldwide income sources in U.S. funds? • Advise IRS of "closer connection" to Canada. • How will second residence acquisitions affect you? • Keep medical receipts for deductability on Canadian return.

This partial checklist of personal events shows you how very important it is to check out the tax consequences of your actions before you make them—*and keep your documentation*. The following chapters will elaborate.

CHAPTER 31
Income Splitting

Under our current tax system, once your taxable income exceeds $29,590, your marginal tax rate goes up dramatically to an average federal/provincial tax rate of 42 per cent from 27 per cent. That's 15 points—and very close to our top average marginal rate of 49 per cent.

This means that all middle and upper-middle income earners should pay careful attention to their tax-filing rights, and in particular the ability to split income to lower earners in the family.

While income splitting is closely monitored by Revenue Canada, it is not illegal. You just need to know the rules.

First, you must know the Attribution Rules. Taxpayers who transfer or loan money to their spouses or minor children must generally report any interest and dividend income on their return. This generally refers to capital that has been earned by the higher-income earner but can work in the reverse also. It means, for example, that if you give your spouse (including a common-law spouse) $20,000 to invest in a GIC, you have to report the interest. The same rule holds true if you buy that GIC in the name of your minor child.

Let's say you take that $20,000 and invest it in a dividend-producing stock in the name of your spouse or child. The resulting dividends must be reported by you.

Capital gains (or losses) on disposition of income-producing assets are treated somewhat differently. In the case of a disposition of property in the name of your spouse but sourcing back to your earnings, the capital gain is reported by you. Capital gains earned on the disposition of capital assets held in the name of your minor children, however, may be reported in the children's hands.

If you invest the $20,000 in a business that your spouse owns and runs, resulting business income will be reported by your spouse. Only capital gains or losses resulting from the disposition of the capital assets of the business will be reportable by you.

The Attribution Rules that extend to transfers of assets to minor children apply whether or not the child is yours. The minor, for example, can be your grandchild, nephew, niece or other child not dealt with "at arm's length." This term refers to someone related to you; someone other than a stranger.

You are considered to be dealing in a "non-arm's length transaction" if you deal with your children, siblings, spouse, in-laws, or any adopted children.

> **MONEY MANAGEMENT TIP 46**
>
> Learn to legally avoid the attribution rules, and split income to the lower-income earner so that it is taxed at lower rates, which will benefit the family unit as a whole.

The key to income splitting, then, is to have the lower-income earners invest, rather than spend, their own income. Resulting investment earnings are then taxed at their lower marginal tax rate.

WAYS TO SPLIT INCOME TO OTHER FAMILY MEMBERS

1. *There is no tax on gifts to your spouse or child.* Only resulting earnings, as described above, must be attributed back to the gift-giver. So, give your spouse or child the money to buy consumer goods, pay for their education or buy a tax-exempt principal residence. Have your dependants use their after-tax dollars to make investments in their own right.

2. *Open bank accounts for your children.* Don't spend the Child Tax Benefit you or your spouse receives; instead, invest it in the name of each child for whom it is paid. Resulting earnings from that investment are taxed to the child. Invest any Goods and Services Tax Credit in the recipient's account. (This should be directed at tax time to be the lower-income earner.)

3. *Invest in a Spousal RRSP.* You get the tax deduction, based on your own RRSP room, but your spouse becomes the annuitant. If the money is left in the plan at least three years from the last spousal contribution, resulting withdrawals are taxed in the hands of the lower-earning spouse.

4. *Pay a salary to your spouse or child.* If your spouse or child works for you in your business, at a reasonable salary or wage that you would pay to a stranger, you can make and deduct such payments as a business expense. The benefits to the family are enormous. The business income is split among family members, each paying tax at a lower rate

than a sole-income earner would. RRSP contribution room is created for each family member, providing for a window of opportunity on tax-sheltered retirement savings. Money must actually be paid for work actually done.

5. *Have the spouse or child reinvest second-generation earnings.* If you had to include the interest or dividends earned on investments you made in the name of your minor spouse or child, have those earnings reinvested in the dependant's name. Earnings generated by investing income that was previously attributed can be reported by the spouse or child.

6. *Make an interest-free business loan.* You can loan money to your spouse to invest in a business, even if you do so on an interest-free basis. The resulting business income will not be attributed back to you.

7. *Make a bona fide investment loan.* You can loan money to your spouse for investment purposes and have resulting income taxed in the spouse's hands, provided that annual interest payments are made to you no later than January 31 after year-end, and at prescribed interest rates. Prescribed interest rates are set every quarter by Revenue Canada, based on 90-day Treasury Bill yields.

8. *Give money to adult children.* The attribution rules generally concern only minor children. Special rules exist if you transfer money to your child who is age 18 or over. If you make an interest-free loan for the purposes of shifting investment income to your child, for example, resulting investment income will be attributed back to you. To avoid this, make a commercial loan, using the prescribed interest rates, as described above. However, if you loan your child money to finance expenditures that do not result in taxable income, such as education costs or the costs of buying a home, no attribution results.

9. *Hold your child's mortgage.* You may be in a position to buy a home for your child. If your child repays you the principal, without interest, there is no tax consequence. The repayment of the capital does not have to be reported by the parent and is not deductible to the child. The benefit arises within the family unit when your child avoids paying non-deductible interest from after-tax dollars. However, if the child repays principal and interest, the interest component is taxable to the parent. This is reverse income splitting. That is, the child who may be in a higher tax bracket pays interest that is received and taxed at his parent's lower tax rate. Any increases in the value of the property are accrued tax free as an exempt principal residence.

10. *Transfer dividends to the higher-income earner.* You can elect to transfer dividend income earned by the lower-income earner to the higher-income earner in order to utilize the dividend tax credit. This transfer can only take place if it increases or creates a Spousal Amount.

CHAPTER 32
How Interest Income Is Taxed

As previously discussed in Part 2, interest income is earned from investments in debt instruments such as GICs, bonds and T-Bills. In general, interest on savings accounts, term deposits and GICs, as well as certain bonds such as Canada Savings Bonds, will be paid out annually as "regular interest" or will be left to compound over time.

Regular interest is paid directly to the investor when it is due. It can be credited to a savings account or paid out of a term deposit or "Regular" Canada Savings Bond in cash. Such interest is reported as income in the year it is paid. Compounding interest is not paid out to the investor. It is credited to the bond and earns interest on the interest as well as the principal.

The rules for compounding investments have been very complex in recent years, with the result that some investors have moved out of compounding, interest-bearing investments such as Canada Savings Bonds altogether. This is a shame, as our discussion of the benefits of compounding has shown that compounding investments result in higher overall returns.

Complex rules pertain to compounding investments that were acquired after 1981 and before 1990. These investments, including Canada Savings Bonds Series 37 to 44, term deposits and life insurance policies that have savings features, had special reporting rules. Compounding interest was required to be reported at least every three years but could, upon election, be reported annually. If you elect to report compounding interest annually, you must "catch up" any unreported accrued interest in the year you switch your methods.

The accrued interest earned must be reported as follows:
- On an annual basis for post-1989 investments.
- At least every three years for post-1981 and pre-1990 investments.
- Pre-1982 investments are considered to have paid interest as at December 31, 1991, and if maturity has not yet been reached, accrue every three years after this.

Consult *Jacks on Tax Savings* for the statistical data required to report interest on Canada Savings Bonds for those who need to make adjustments to prior filed tax returns.

While those are the general rules for the reporting of interest income, following are some specific tips:

Canada Savings Bonds

Series 27 to 41 have matured. Check your safety deposit box to make sure none is left pining somewhere. They are not earning interest and inflation is eating away at their purchasing power. Adjustment for income inclusion might be allowed on some of these old bonds, back to the 1985 tax year. Remember, the 1991 tax year is the one that any interest accrued on pre-1982 bonds was to have been reported, and for the years 1985 to 1987, the $1,000 interest and dividends deduction was still with us.

Series 42 to 44 bonds are the pre-1990 issues that are still "active":
- Report compounding interest on Series 42 annually—if you have so elected—but at least every three years: 1990, 1993, 1996 and 1997 (year of maturity).
- Series 43 must be reported on a triennial basis in 1991, 1994, 1997 and 1998 (year of maturity).
- Series 44 must be reported on a triennial basis in 1992, 1995, 1998 and 2001 (year of maturity).
- Series 45 and future bonds are reported annually and a T-Slip will be issued to record the accrued interest amounts. Be sure the Bank of Canada has your correct address.

Foreign Interest Income

Foreign interest income must be converted to Canadian dollars and reported on the Canadian tax return. The conversion rate to be used is usually that at the date of receipt of funds, although Revenue Canada will allow an "average annual conversion rate" in practice. The following chart lists rates in effect on U.S. dollars since 1985:

AVERAGE CONVERSION RATES: U.S.$								
1985	1986	1987	1988	1989	1990	1991	1992	1993
1.3651	1.3894	1.3260	1.2309	1.1842	1.1668	1.1458	1.2083	1.2829

Usually, when foreign income is received, an amount for taxes will be withheld from your income before it is sent to you by the foreign institution. Any foreign taxes you pay can be used in the calculation of the "foreign tax credit" on Schedule 1 of the T1 General return. This calculation allows you to recover some or all of your foreign tax paid. The full amount of interest is reported as income.

In the event that the foreign tax credit does not recover all of the foreign taxes you paid, the balance can be recovered through a special calculation. In this instance, claim a deduction for the excess foreign tax paid as a "carrying charge." This is claimable on line 229 of the tax return.

Alternately, you may simply reduce the foreign income earned by the amount of the taxes paid, and claim the net foreign income on the Canadian return. You might do this if you were otherwise not able to use the foreign tax credit to your advantage—perhaps if your income was too low or other provisions, such as the amount of your non-refundable tax credits, dividend tax credits or minimum tax carryovers, reduce the federal taxes payable. This method will, in some cases, increase or create a Spousal Credit.

If you are earning compounding interest, you will be required to use the triennial reporting rules, as usual, if the investment was acquired prior to 1990, or the mandatory annual reporting for investments acquired after 1989. Because the foreign tax credit is only payable when the interest is actually paid and taxes are actually withheld, you may wish to file a "waiver" to keep your tax returns open beyond the normal three-year assessment period for these items only. Such a waiver is filed on Form T2029, and should be discussed with your tax advisor.

Treasury Bills

T-Bills are acquired at a discount. When they mature at par, the difference between what you paid for the bill and what you received is considered to be interest income. If you do not hold the T-Bills to maturity, a capital gain or loss could be incurred on the disposition of them.

Fees paid to a broker for handling of your T-Bill transactions usually will be considered on account of capital. However, because the income is considered fully taxable if the T-Bill is held to maturity, there may be a case for writing off the fees as a carrying charge on line 229 of the T1 General.

Bonds

Special tax treatment is given to government bonds that are issued at a discount. These rules are also fairly complex. The federal government wants bondholders to pre-report interest accrued on these bonds on an annual basis, if acquired after 1989, and at least on a triennial basis, if acquired after 1981 and before 1990. If there is an over-reporting of the accrued interest, a deduction will be available for the year of disposition. Again, if the bond is not held to maturity, a capital gain or loss on disposition occurs.

When you buy a bond, there is another important factor to watch for. Sometimes interest has accrued to the date of purchase. You, as the purchaser, must pay any interest accrued to the vendor because you will reap the proceeds later when the bond matures. Any such interest paid by the purchaser can be deducted as a carrying charge on the tax return. The vendor, of course, must report such interest as income.

> **MONEY MANAGEMENT TIP 47**
>
> Keep meticulous records of the interest-accruing investments you own to avoid double reporting on your income tax return.

Never Double Report

In conclusion, keep track of how much interest is being reported under these accrual rules. They are so complex that we have seen large and expensive errors on T5-Slips issued by certain financial institutions in Canada. If you are receiving a T5-Slip every year for accrued interest, be sure to match such pre-reported interest to the payout you receive on maturity of the debt instrument. Some companies have reported 100 per cent of the interest received in the year of maturity instead of only the one year annual reporting that was required. This means that unsuspecting taxpayers paid tax twice on their interest earnings.

Don't let this happen to you. Keep on top of how much interest you are pre-reporting, particularly if you have a large investment portfolio.

How to compute your after-tax yield.

If you have investment income earnings, compute your after-tax yield as follows:

Current yield × (1 minus your marginal tax rate) = After-tax yield

So, if your current yield is 6 per cent and your marginal tax rate is 42 per cent, then your after-tax yield is only 3.48 per cent.

6% × (1 − .42)
6% ×   .58   = .0348

You must really make 10.35 per cent on the investment to get a true after-tax return of 6 per cent. That is:

$$\frac{\text{Investment yield}}{1 - \text{marginal tax rate}} = \text{Before-tax yield needed}$$

$$\frac{.06}{.58} = 10.35\%$$

How to compute your after tax after inflation results

In the previous example, we know we'll reap only 3.48 per cent on our 6 per cent investment once we take into consideration our marginal tax rate. Now we must still account for inflation. Here's how:

Real Rate ≃ Nominal Rate less Expected Rate of Inflation
3.5%   ≃   6%   −   2.5%

Unfortunately, as shown above, Revenue Canada taxes us on the nominal rate of 6%, not the real rate after inflation. So, to account for inflation on our after tax return of .0348, we must subtract the inflation rate of 2.5%. What do we keep on an after-tax, after-inflation basis?

Only .98%!

If you wanted an after-tax, real rate of return of 6%:

$$\frac{\text{Real Rate of Return} + \text{Expected Rate of Inflation}}{(1 - \text{Marginal Tax Rate})}$$

$$\frac{6\% + 2.5\%}{1 - .42} = \frac{8.50}{0.58} = 14.6552\%$$

To break even after tax and inflation:

$$\frac{\text{Expected inflation rate}}{1 - \text{marginal tax}} \quad \frac{2.50}{0.58} = 4.31\%$$

Special thanks to Professor Larry A. Wood, Faculty of Management, University of Calgary for his assistance with these calculations. He notes: "Calculating the real rate as merely the nominal rate minus the expected rate of inflation is an over simplification that ignores the "Fisher Effect," which dictates

$$\text{Real Rate of Return} = \left[\left(\frac{1 + \text{Nominal Rate of Return}}{1 + \text{Expected Rate of Inflation}}\right) - 1\right]$$

CHAPTER 33
Interest Deductibility

Should you borrow money to make your investments? This will largely depend on the return you are expecting from the investment, the amount of risk you are taking in borrowing the money, your tax rate, and whether the investments are made in a registered (i.e., RRSP) or non-registered account.

> **MONEY MANAGEMENT TIP 48**
> Write off the interest expenses you pay on money borrowed to earn income from a business or property held outside of your RRSP.

Interest expenses are generally tax deductible if the money was borrowed to earn income from a business or property. There are a few exceptions. For example, if you borrow money to buy an RRSP or to contribute to a Registered Pension Plan or Deferred Profit-Sharing Plan, the interest is not deductible. Also, if you borrow money to buy a piece of undeveloped land, the interest is not deductible and will be added to the cost of the land so that any future capital gains are reduced. If a portion of the income-producing asset is transferred to personal use, interest also ceases to be tax deductible.

Therefore, if you borrow money to acquire a common stock, the interest is tax deductible because taxable income is expected in the form of dividends in the long run. The same logic applies if you acquire debt obligations that pay interest. In fact, interest is deductible when it is either paid or "payable" as long as you follow a consistent method of reporting. Therefore, if interest payments were due but not paid, you may still be able to make a tax deduction if you follow an "accrual method" of reporting interest.

If your interest deduction exceeds your income, the net loss can be used to offset other income of the year. So, if your investment reaps no income over a period of time, the interest costs themselves would be paid in part by the tax savings you would reap by writing off the interest deduction.

Taxpayers who hold equity in a home can turn non-deductible mortgage interest into deductible interest. If you take out a mortgage on the property and use that money to invest in an income-producing business or property, the interest you pay becomes tax deductible. If you are successful in preserving the principal amount and earning a return on your investment, your gamble has paid off. If your investment turns sour, you are stuck paying down your new mortgage, but with the consolation that the interest is now deductible.

Margin Accounts

Investors can get "credit" from their investment dealer or buy securities on "margin" if there is acceptable security (usually the asset you buy). The amount that you pay to buy the asset is called the "margin;" interest is charged by your broker on the balance owed on credit. Be forewarned, though, that if the value of the assets drops in price, the brokerage firm can require you to put more money into the pot. When this happens, there is a "margin call." If you can't put in more money, the broker can sell the securities, at a loss if necessary.

New Rules for Interest Deductibility

Interest expenses incurred after 1987 to acquire a property used to earn income will be deductible in equal portions over a five-year period, starting the year the expenses were incurred. This new rule will also be allowed in cases where debt is rescheduled or restructured on income-producing assets. Financing charges that relate only to the year they are incurred will be deductible in that year.

Loss of Source of Income

Interest normally ceases to be deductible when the source of income to which the charges relate no longer exist and/or the borrowed money cannot be traced to another income-producing source. Under new rules introduced with the February 22, 1994 budget, it is proposed that where the loss of source of income occurs after 1993, interest on borrowed money will continue to be deductible under certain circumstances. Any portion of interest expenses traceable to personal use will not be tax deductible.

So, if you borrowed money to buy a capital asset other than real or depreciable property, and you lose a portion of this property due to a decline in value, interest expenses will continue to be tax deductible.

Break-even Points

Borrowing money can be a good way to multiply your investment returns. However, always consider the net return of your activities and compare that to the risk of owing money. Compute your break-even point, after tax and interest payable, before you make the decision to borrow. Have your tax accountant prepare a preliminary calculation of the net tax results of your proposed transaction. You must earn more than the rate of interest you are paying to come out ahead after inflation. Think about it.

CHAPTER 34 Taxation of Dividend Income

If you are earning dividend income, you are paying the least possible tax on your investment income. This is because dividends are a distribution of after-tax profits of the corporation—the government has already made money on the corporate profits themselves.

As an individual shareholder, you win because of the "dividend tax credit" mechanism.

Let's assume your taxable income is $40,000. Your marginal tax rate is 42 per cent. When you add a $100 dividend to your income, you must "gross it up" by 25 per cent to $125.

Remember, you actually only received $100. Now you are increasing your net income by $125. This will affect your provincial net income taxes (where applicable), your Child Tax Benefits (if available), medical expense claims, charitable donation claims and other provisions affected by the size of your net income.

The amount of tax payable on your $125 extra income is $52.50 (42 per cent of $125). However, you are entitled to a dividend tax credit of 20 per cent of $125 ($25.00). (This is a combined federal/provincial dividend tax credit of 20 per cent—13.33 per cent times 1.50)

The result is that the net taxes payable on your dividend of $100 is $27.50. If this $100 received was in the form of interest, you would have paid 42 per cent of $100 or $42.00. Earning dividends puts $14.50 more in your pocket on an after-tax basis.

EARNING TAX-FREE DIVIDENDS

If you had no other income, except for dividend payments, you could receive up to $20,000 virtually tax free under this mechanism. The $20,000 would be grossed up to $25,000, and the offsetting dividend tax credit (federal/provincial) would approximate $5,000. Therefore, the tax on $25,000—which at an average federal/provincial rate of 27 per cent is $6,750—would be reduced by the $5,000 dividend tax credit and your personal non-refundable credits of about $1,743 (27 per cent of $6,456 for a single taxpayer) for a net tax liability of $7.00.

Any amount of dividends earned over and above this level will result in a tax liability.

Here are a few more points you should know about "dividends:"

1. If you are a high-income earner subject to the *Minimum Tax*, add only the actual amount of dividends to the calculation, not the grossed-up amount. Accordingly, no dividend tax credit is allowed.

2. *Foreign dividends* received are not grossed up and do not qualify for the dividend tax credit. However, they must be reported in Canadian dollars.

3. *Stock dividends* amount to extra shares received out of the corporation instead of a cash payment of dividends. In this case, if the amounts were received after May 24, 1985, stock dividends become taxable to the extent of their "paid up capital." Such stock dividends are treated like ordinary dividends and become taxable in the normal manner when received. Later, any increase in value over the paid-up capital will be subject to the normal capital gains rules upon disposition.

4. *Stock splits* will not be taxable at all until there is a disposition.

5. *Capital gains dividends* are a distribution of capital gains, usually from a mutual fund and receive capital gains treatment.

6. *Capital dividends*, paid out of the Capital Dividend Account of a private corporation, usually holds the non-taxable portion of capital gains realized by the company since 1971. These dividends are not taxable, and no adjustment is made to the adjusted cost base of the shares.

7. *Deemed dividends* resulting from corporate reorganizations or share redemptions will be treated like ordinary dividends except in the case of

Class I Special Shares of Reed Stenhouse Companies Limited issued before January 1, 1986. When these shares are redeemed, capital gains treatment will result.

8. *Dividends earned by the lower-income spouse* may be transferred and reported as income by the higher earner if by doing so a Spousal Amount is created or increased. Work out both tax returns in both ways to determine if there is a benefit to the transfer.

9. *Patronage dividends* are payments made to customers of a co-op or other company in amounts that depend upon the amount of money spent in the store. These amounts are usually shown on a T4A Slip and are taxed in full unless the purchases are business-related. In that case, patronage dividends on net consumer goods are taxable only.

10. There are certain dividends that are non-taxable. These dividends will reduce adjusted cost base of the shares held and therefore increase any capital gain on disposition. These include the following:

    - The Algoma Steel Corporation, Limited, 8% Tax-Deferred Preference Shares, Series A.
    - Aluminum Company of Canada, Limited, $2.00 Tax-Deferred Retractable Preferred Shares.
    - Brascan Limited, 8.5% Tax-Deferred Preferred Shares, Series A.
    - Canada Permanent Mortgage Corporation, 6.75% Tax-Deferred Convertible Preference Shares Series A.
    - Cominco Limited, $2.00 Tax-Deferred Exchangeable Preferred Shares Series A.

MONEY MANAGEMENT TIP 49

Earn dividends from your investments in capital stock, for the best after-tax return available.

CHAPTER 35
Capital Gains and Losses

A capital gain or loss will only occur when you sell, transfer or otherwise "dispose" of your capital assets, as explained in Chapter 27. Your capital assets that may give rise to a capital gain or loss will include the following:

1. Qualified small business corporation shares.
2. Qualified farm property.
3. Real estate.
4. Depreciable properties.
5. Bonds, debentures, promissory notes.
6. Personal-use properties.
7. Listed personal properties.
8. Eligible capital properties.
9. Other securities or shares.

The tax consequences of dispositions of these properties can vary. Qualified small business corporation shares, for example, are listed separately because capital gains on these properties will qualify for the Super Capital Gains Exemption of $500,000, while losses due to insolvency qualify for special tax treatment under the "Business Investment Loss Rules."

Gains arising from the disposition of qualified farm properties also qualify for the Super Exemption, while losses can be carried back three years and forward indefinitely. Special tax-free rollover provisions apply when farm property is transferred to spouse, children or grandchildren.

Real estate gains can be classified as either on account of "income" or "capital," depending on circumstances, while depreciable property dispositions will not result in capital losses as such events are handled on the capital cost allowance schedule.

Bonds, debentures and promissory notes may have both an "interest income" and a capital component on disposition, while personal-use properties have special rules relating to dispositions at a loss (described below).

Eligible capital properties such as goodwill in a business, or franchises, trademarks licenses or customer lists are intangible assets. These assets are entered on the capital cost allowance statement at three-quarters (3/4) of their cost and then depreciated at a 7 per cent rate. Dispositions which result in a negative balance may receive capital gains treatment.

Other capital properties, include dispositions of shares of common stock or any other property that doesn't fall into a special category described above.

In its simplest form, a capital gain or loss is calculated as follows:

Proceeds of Disposition (less) Adjusted Cost Base (less)Outlays and Expenses = Capital Gain or Loss

Proceeds of Disposition are usually the sales price. However, what if you disposed of the property without selling it? This might occur upon death, or when you convert an asset from business to personal use. In such cases, the fair market value (FMV) of the property at date of disposition is used as the "proceeds."

Adjusted Cost Base is what you paid for the asset, or the fair market value at the time it was transferred to you, plus any additions and improvements. It can also be one of a number of different "V-Days" or Valuation Days. Increases in values of certain assets are taxable only after V-Day.

The increases in values of assets were not taxed at all before 1972. This is why we have two V-Days in that year: one for publicly traded shares, and one for all other properties.

VALUATION DAYS FOR THE PURPOSES OF CALCULATING ADJUSTED COST BASE

December 22, 1971: Valuation day for publicly traded shares in Canada.

December 31, 1971: The last day before capital gains became taxable in Canada.

December 31, 1981: The day before accrued gains in second residences became subject to tax.

February 22, 1994: The day used for deemed dispositions of capital assets for purposes of crystallizing any unused capital gains deductions.

The 1981 V-Day is specific to second personal residences. Before 1982, each spouse could own one tax-exempt personal residence; thereafter, the family unit could only own one. This means that a valuation of the properties is necessary as at December 31, 1981, so as to determine which one should be considered the exempt residence and which should be the "taxable" residence.

On January 1, 1993, common-law unions became subject to the same rules as legally married couples have. That meant that gains in second family residences in those instances became subject to the capital gains tax rules.

MONEY MANAGEMENT TIP 50

Use the one-time opportunity to pre-report accrued gains on the 1994 tax return to use up any available capital gains deduction you or your family members may still have.

Finally, the February 22, 1994, V-Day refers to the date used in generating "deemed gains" for the purposes of utilizing the $100,000 Capital Gains Deduction, which was eliminated as of that day. For the 1994 tax year only, taxpayers may take a value anywhere between adjusted cost base and the FMV of their properties as at February 22, 1994 and pre-report any capital gains accrued in this time. They will then use the offsetting capital gains deduction on their 1994 return for the last time.

Adjusted cost base can be increased by all legal fees and brokerage fees paid to acquire the asset. To this you can add the cost of any improvements to the property made during the time you owned it (such as putting a new addition onto the cottage).

Outlays and Expenses are the costs of disposing of the property, such as real estate commissions, brokerage fees and advertising costs. Once adjusted cost base and outlays and expenses are deducted from the proceeds, a capital gain or loss will result.

Capital gains or losses are not fully taxable. In fact, the income "inclusion rate" has changed over the years:

INCOME INCLUSION RATES FOR CAPITAL GAINS	
1972-1987	50.00%
1988-1989	66.67%
1990 forward	75.00%

Therefore, the "taxable portion" of your capital gain incurred on dispositions after 1990 is 75 per cent. The same rules are applied when there are decreases in the value of an asset over its original cost. In such cases a "capital loss" occurs.

Capital losses are used to reduce other capital gains of the year. There is only one exception to this rule, and that is on personal-use property losses.

Losses on your personal-use properties—your home, cottage, car, boat, furniture, etc. are not deductible at all. They are borne personally. Gains on personal use properties are also subject to a special "$1,000 Rule." That is, proceeds of disposition and adjusted cost base of the properties are deemed to be at least $1,000, so that tax consequences only exist on dispositions of larger items valued over this amount.

Example 1
Elliott sells his boat, which he acquired for $900 in 1990, for $750. There is no tax consequence because proceeds and adjusted cost base are each deemed to be $1,000.

Example 2
Elliott sells his dining-room table, which he purchased for $600 in 1992, for $1,250. In this case, there is a capital gain of $250. Adjusted cost base is deemed to be $1,000, and the proceeds are $1,250.

Example 3
Elliott sells his cottage, which he acquired for $50,000 in 1991, for $45,000. Even though there is a loss, it is a personal-use property loss which is not deductible on the tax return at all.

The "$1,000 Rule" also applies to the category of property known as "Listed Personal Property." This category includes personal use assets that normally appreciate in value such as antiques, rare books, stamps, coins, art, jewellery, etc. In this category, listed personal property losses can be used to reduce other listed personal property gains only. Unused losses can be carried back and applied against other listed personal property gains of the prior three years, or carried forward and applied in similar fashion for seven years.

Other Capital Losses

For other categories of capital property, loss application rules are the following: If there are no other capital gains in the year a capital loss occurs, three-quarters of the loss, known as the "allowable capital loss," can be carried back for up to three tax years to reduce capital gains incurred in that time, or carried forward indefinitely to reduce future capital gains. Careful tracking of this information is therefore necessary. Capital losses incurred after May 24, 1985 can no longer be used to reduce other income of the year. If you incurred a loss on the disposition of shares or debt of a small business corporation through insolvency or bankruptcy, such "Allowable Business Investment Losses" will receive special treatment (described in Chapter 36.)

For a detailed discussion of the tax calculations of the asset types itemized above, please see *Jacks on Tax Savings*. See Chapter 40 below for a discussion of the capital gains deduction.

In terms of your investment assets, there are some special rules. You may wish to discuss these with your tax practitioner:

1. *Identical properties.* When you hold shares of the same company, capital gains or losses are calculated when any one of the shares are sold. In such cases, calculate the adjusted cost base of the shares you are selling as the average cost of all the identical shares. Bonds, bills, notes or debentures will be treated as identical properties if all rights are identical.

2. *More than one use.* When a capital property has both a business and a personal use, the cost of the property is divided according to its percentage use in earning income from a business or property. That way, future capital gains or losses are allocated directly to its business usage. Dispositions at fair market value can also be calculated if the asset is later converted entirely to personal use.

3. *Commodity futures.* If you are a speculator trading in commodities, including wheat, corn, potatoes, copper, silver, pork bellies, lumber and others, your gains or losses could be ruled as ordinary income if you are in the business of trading in that particular commodity, or if you have access to information through your employment about the commodity you are trading in.

4. *Transactions not considered to be dispositions.* When you enter into a transaction for the purpose of securing a debt or loan, and a transfer of legal ownership takes place for this purpose, no disposition of capital property is considered to have taken place, and therefore no capital gains or losses must be reported.

5. *Transfers of property to a charity.* If you give capital property to a charity, you may elect a value between adjusted cost base and fair market value at the time of transfer as the proceeds of disposition. The resulting capital gain is reported on the tax return, and an offsetting charitable donations credit can be taken, subject to a maximum credit of 20 per cent of net income. Excess donations are carried forward for a five-year period, always subject to the 20 per cent of net income rule. Capital losses cannot be generated under this special provision, because the fair market value must exceed the adjusted cost base. This would also be true of any recapture or terminal loss.

If you should give a gift of cultural property to a designated institution that is certified by the Canadian Cultural Property Export Review Board, you will be entitled to a donations tax credit of its certified fair market value. Capital gains arising from such transactions will not be taxable, and the 20 per cent of net income limitation will not be used. Capital losses will be treated in the normal fashion. Reporters, broadcasters, media representatives are among those persons who should be keeping stock of the history-making documents they may possess for future donation to a university or other institution.

6. *Changes in terms of debt securities.* A disposition will be considered to take place if a security changes from interest-bearing to non-interest bearing or vice versa, or if there is a change in maturity dates or repayment schedules. A disposition is also considered to have taken place if the debtor changes, or where there is an increase or decrease in the principal amount owed.

7. *Changes in terms of shares.* A disposition will normally be considered to have occurred if there is a change in voting control, or a change in preferred share values, or a change to make them cumulative from non-cumulative or vice versa, unless the original terms of agreement provided for such instances. The February 24, 1994 budget proposed that a rollover without tax consequences may be available in cases where the paid-up capital of the classes of shares received on exchange will be reduced.

8. *Corporate reorganizations.* When two companies merge, a new set of shares is usually issued to shareholders in the newly merged company. The old shares are considered to be sold at fair market value, and the new shares acquired at their fair market value. All of the normal tax consequences will result. In some cases, however, the shares are considered to have been sold and acquired at the adjusted cost base of the old shares. Check the share documentation of the newly merged company carefully to avoid tax consequences in these instances.

9. *Receipt of Treasury shares.* If you receive treasury shares in exchange for shares of another corporation, you may be considered to have disposed of the old shares at their adjusted cost base. This treatment would defer any capital gains or losses to the time of disposition of the new shares. Discuss the option to treat your transaction in this manner with your tax professional. It may be to your advantage to report the disposition of the old shares at fair market value, in the normal manner.

10. *Election on Canadian Securities.* The first time you report a disposition of Canadian Securities, you may elect to have all gains and losses from such transactions to be treated as capital gains or losses. This optional election is not open to you if you are a non-resident or a dealer or trader in securities. This election would apply to future dispositions of any capital stock, debentures, notes, mortgages, bonds or other obligations issued by a company resident in Canada. Speak to your tax advisor about filing Form T123.

11. *Superficial losses.* Investors often generate "tax losses" at year-end by selling losers in their portfolio to offset capital gains they have generated. This is legitimate and should be discussed with your investment broker. However, if you turn around and repurchase an identical security within 30 days before or after a sale, any loss created by the transactions will be considered "superficial" and not deductible.

12. *Deferring gains where possible.* Capital gains and losses must be reported on the tax return in the calendar year in which they occur. This is true even of capital gains or losses that occur within your proprietorship, which may have a different fiscal year-end. Therefore, if you are selling securities at year end, remember that capital gains that are generated in January of the new year, as opposed to December, will not be reported until next year's return is filed—a full 15 months away. This can be very important in light of the removal of the $100,000 Capital Gains Deduction and if your marginal tax rate is expected to drop in the new year.

CHAPTER 36
Special Rules When Things Go Wrong

The recession of the early 1990s felled many a company. The tax consequences of insolvency or uncollectible debts are important, as they may have lucrative tax benefits for you when your affairs improve.

Capital losses, as outlined previously, can be applied against other capital gains of the year. Excess losses can be carried back and applied against capital gains in the previous three tax years. This allows you to reach back and recover taxes already paid on gains that may have been taxable in a year of high income. You can also choose to carry unapplied losses forward indefinitely into the future.

UNCOLLECTIBLE TRADE DEBTS

If you are owed money by someone, the tax consequences can vary. For example, uncollectible trade debts are fully deductible under your business income. Losses arising from uncollectible non-interest-bearing loans will not be deductible at all, unless the amounts were given to a corporation in which you are a shareholder or a partnership in which you are a partner, and the organization has since ceased operations.

Uncollectible amounts originating from the *disposition of depreciable property* (property upon which depreciation has been claimed) require some special adjustments. At the time the asset was disposed of, you would have indicated the disposition on the capital cost allowance schedule, and a reduction in the value of the pool of assets would have resulted. If the asset disposed of was the last asset of the class, terminal loss or recapture would have resulted.

If those proceeds later become uncollectible, you may be able to take both an income deduction and a capital loss. For example, let's say you sold your office furniture and fixtures, which you acquired for $5,000, for a total sum of $4,000. You collected $1,000 and the balance became uncollectible. On your tax return you would take a deduction from income of $3,000, which is the lesser of:

The uncollectible proceeds	$3,000
Capital cost less any amounts collected	$4,000

The undeducted $1,000 that is left on the bad debt is treated as a capital loss. If there is any recovery of the debt in the future, such amounts would have to be added to the income and capital accounts in the same proportion as deducted above.

FORGIVEN DEBTS

If you previously borrowed money for an income-producing purpose, and found yourself unable to pay back the debt, special tax treatment will apply if you were able to settle the debt for an amount less than the principal, or the amount was forgiven altogether.

First you must calculate the amount remaining after payment (if any) to settle the debt. For example, let's say that Jonas owed his bank $50,000 on an income-producing loan, and was able to settle it for $25,000. The excess, $25,000, is now used to reduce the following items:

- non-capital losses of prior years
- farm losses of prior years
- net capital losses of prior years
- restricted farm losses of prior years
- cumulative Canadian development expenses
- cumulative Canadian oil and gas property expense
- undepreciated capital cost of depreciable property
- cumulative eligible capital
- the adjusted cost base of any non-depreciable property owned.

If there is still unapplied debt, it must now be added to income, if the debt was settled after February 21, 1994. Special reserve may be claimed to include such amounts only to the extent of 20% of income over $40,000. In cases where shares of the capital stock of a corporation are substituted for debt, the debt is considered to have been settled for a payment equal to the fair market value of the share at that time.

These rules have the effect of reducing future tax deductions, or increasing future capital gains, first. They will not apply to someone who is bankrupt, or if the debt is forgiven through a will.

Mortgage foreclosures are treated under separate rules discussed in Chapter 39.

DEBT GUARANTEES

If you guarantee a loan for someone, you are considered to have acquired a debt when you are called upon to fulfil your obligations as the guarantor. If your guarantee was given for the purposes of earning income, the rules described above will apply. The guarantor may qualify for special treatment under allowable business investment loss rules described below, if the guarantee was made at "arm's length" (not to a relative or related corporation). The guarantee must have been called within 12 months of cessation of business.

INSOLVENT SMALL BUSINESS CORPORATIONS

If you had a share or debt of a small business corporation, and those debts become uncollectible or the company becomes insolvent or bankrupt, you will be considered to have incurred a capital loss that is treated as an "allowable business investment loss." Three-quarters of such losses may be deducted from other income of the year on line 217 of the T1 General return. If the amount of the loss exceeds your other income of the year, any excess becomes a "non-capital loss" that can be carried back and applied to other income of the previous three years, and carried forward and applied to other income of the next seven years. Excesses still remaining after this time become "capital losses" in the seventh year. Such losses can only be applied against capital gains of the year, carried back and used against capital losses of the previous three years (although the non-capital loss provisions should make this unnecessary) and carried forward indefinitely.

A small business corporation is a Canadian Controlled Private Corporation that carries on active business in Canada, using 90 per cent or more of the fair market value of its assets in such an active business.

The allowable business investment losses will be reduced by any previously claimed capital gains deduction. Any such reduction becomes a capital loss that is eligible for the normal rules.

OTHER INSOLVENT CORPORATIONS

If you dispose of shares of a corporation that does not qualify as a small business corporation at a loss, you will have incurred a capital loss. This is calculated as the difference between what you acquired the shares for, and nil proceeds. This treatment would generally apply to losses on public corporations or private ones that do not meet the "active business" rules described earlier.

If an insolvent corporation is revived, a capital gain may result if the company carries on business within a 24-month period. In this situation, seek out the expertise of your tax professional.

REFINANCING

New rules introduced with the February 22, 1994 budget will allow taxpayers to continue to write off interest charges where loans continue to be paid off in cases where a business has ceased. See previous comments on interest deductibility in Chapter 33.

> **MONEY MANAGEMENT TIP 51**
>
> New rules allow for continuing deductibility of interest expenses in cases of insolvency. Consult your tax professional to determine the consequences of any refinancing you may be attempting.

CHAPTER 37
Inside or Outside an RRSP

Missing links—that's what some people have when it comes to their RRSPs. They know they should be contributing to one although they don't always understand why, how much or what investments they should choose for it. In addition, it's become apparent to me recently that many average Canadians do not understand the difference between investing inside an RRSP and investing outside of an RRSP.

There is a critical difference that has tax side-effects. First, let's clarify when and why you want to invest in an RRSP. You can only invest in an RRSP if you have "earned income" from a prior year. You'd like to invest in one because you have "taxable income" in the current tax year that can be reduced by an RRSP deduction. And you want to do this because the RRSP will pay you an immediate return on your investment of 28 per cent to 52 per cent, depending on your tax bracket, through tax deductions.

"Earned income" is actively pursued: employment income (net of any refunds of such income, union or professional dues or employment expenses), net self-employment income (reduced by any losses claimed), net rental income (reduced by any losses), alimony or maintenance payments received (reduced by any amounts deducted or repaid), net research grants, royalties earned by an author or inventor, to name a few.

You must have the following "earning income" levels—last year—to maximize your annual RRSP contribution:

Tax Year	Maximum Contribution	Earned Income Required	In Year
1991	$11,500	$63,889	1990
1992	$12,500	$69,444	1991
1993	$12,500	$69,444	1992
1994	$13,500	$75,000	1993
1995	$14,500	$80,556	1994
1996	$15,500	$86,111	1995

There is a reason we are repeating prior year contribution maximums for you, which is to point out that if you could not afford to—or for some other reason did not—contribute to an RRSP in the past couple of years, your "unused room" could be carried forward to be used in a future year. This carry forward opportunity exists for seven years. That is, you can carry forward unused RRSP room from 1991 until 1998, 1992 room until 1999, and so on.

An additional note on the maximum contributions: the figures shown above are the maximum dollar limits for each tax year indicated. However, taxpayers are restricted to contribute no more than the lesser of the dollar limitation indicated above or 18 per cent of their "earned income" in the prior year, less any Pension Adjustment (PA) indicated on last year's T4 (Box 52) or T4A (Box 34) and any Past Service Pension Adjustment for the current tax year. Last year's Notice of Assessment from Revenue Canada will tell you how much room you have to contribute to your RRSP for this tax year.

MONEY MANAGEMENT TIP 52

Find out what RRSP room you have by consulting last year's Notice of Assessment from Revenue Canada.

The only thing it will not tell you is how much you can contribute over and above your room for special transfers such as rollovers of pension income to your spouse's RRSP to a maximum of $6,000, or eligible retiring allowances received from your employer, or refunds of premiums received on death of a spouse.

So let's say you were eligible to contribute the maximum dollar amounts in every year from 1991, 1992 and 1993 (a total of $36,500), but only managed to scratch together $5,500 to contribute in that time. This means you may be able to make a contribution of $31,000 in 1994 if you want to. How much would this deduction be worth to you? Well, at a 50 per cent tax bracket: $15,500.*

This is "new capital" that can now be invested elsewhere to help you build your wealth accumulations.

By the way, if you borrowed to maximize your RRSP contribution, the interest, unfortunately, is not tax deductible. So use your tax savings to pay down your loan first.

TYPES OF RRSPS

There are two types of RRSPs you can invest in. One type is offered by a financial institution, such as a bank or trust company, which will usually invest your money in a GIC or other term deposit. These deposits are guaranteed by the government up to $60,000, under the Canadian Deposit Insurance Corporation.

The other is a "self-administered plan." Under this type of a plan you direct, through a special "RRSP account," where your money is to be invested. It is usually administered by a stock brokerage or like firm which has the ability to acquire and dispose of both fixed- and variable-income investments for you.

> **MONEY MANAGEMENT TIP 53**
>
> Be sure to contribute to an RRSP any time you have the required contribution room in order to earn tax-sheltered investment returns and an immediate return on the tax savings you'll reap.

FEATURES OF INVESTMENTS MADE INSIDE AN RRSP

Investments made into an RRSP are tax sheltered in two ways. First, when you invest the principle sums in an RRSP, you receive a tax deduction, as

---

* Note: Maximum deduction claimed may not exceed 7/2 of current-year dollar maximum

explained above. Second, while your money is invested under the "RRSP Umbrella," you will never pay tax on their earnings—interest, dividends or capital gains—until you withdraw funds out of the RRSP.

Second, investments inside an RRSP lose their identity. Dividends, interest, capital gains and losses all intermingle to give you a net value in the RRSP. You will not be entitled to a dividend tax credit, capital gains treatment or annual accrual requirements for interest earnings. Simply, principal and interest are taxed in full upon withdrawal.

SOME QUALIFYING INVESTMENTS UNDER THE RRSP UMBRELLA
"Registered Funds"

Fixed Income

GICs
T-Bills
Strips
Preferred Shares
Government of Canada Bonds
Certain Provincial Bonds
   (i.e., Manitoba, Saskatchewan)
Mortgages

Variable Income

Certain Mutual Funds
Common Stock of companies listed on prescribed Canadian or foreign stock exchanges
Credit Union Shares
Mutual Funds of companies listed on foreign stock exchanges
Rights/Warrants
Shares in prescribed active Canadian corporations' shares of
Venture Capital Corporations

SOME INVESTMENTS OUTSIDE OF AN RRSP
"Non-Registered Funds"

Fixed Income

GICs
T-Bills
Strips
Preferred Shares
Bonds
Certain Provincial Bonds
Mortgages

Variable Income

Common Stock
Credit Unions
Mutual Funds of Companies Listed on Foreign Stock Exchanges
Rights/Warrants
Shares in Venture Capital Corporations
*Precious Metals
*Real Estate
*Shares of Private Corporations in which you own more than 10 per cent
*Art/Antiques
*Commodity Futures

FEATURES OF INVESTMENTS MADE OUTSIDE OF AN RRSP

- *Choose the same investments—inside or out.* With the exception of the items marked by a star, which are not qualifying investment to an RRSP, you can see that most investments that can be made inside an RRSP can also be made outside an RRSP.
- *No Tax Sheltering.* For non-registered investments, any earnings—interest, dividends or capital gains—are subject to tax, under normal rules. And remember, when you put your money into an investment outside of an RRSP, you will not get a tax deduction for that contribution.
- *No Earned Income Limitation.* Any time you invest outside of an RRSP you have very few restrictions. Perhaps the only restrictions are minimum investment requirements. Outside the RRSP you can invest any disposable income you may have, even if you have no "earned income."

HOW TO MOVE INVESTMENTS INTO AN RRSP

1. Contribute cash directly into the qualifying investment vehicle of your choice.
2. Transfer assets held outside of the RRSP into the RRSP. However, this generates a tax consequence:

    a. Any interest earned and unreported at date of transfer must be included in income.

    b. Securities are considered disposed of at the time you make the contribution and the appropriate tax treatment for capital gains is required. *Capital losses will be deemed to be nil.* Calculate your proceeds of disposition based on the fair market value at the time of transfer.

Next time you think you are too broke to contribute to an RRSP, review your personal net worth statement. Is there any qualifying investment "inventory" that can be moved into your RRSP?

Let's say, for example, that you had $8,500 in RRSP room, but no cash on hand. However, you do have 500 shares of XYZ Company which you acquired last year for $4,000 and $2,000 in Canada Savings Bonds. The accrued interest on the CSBs is $195. You can choose to transfer the XYZ shares into your RRSP at their fair market value ($5,000), as well as the Canada Savings Bonds of $2,000, for a total investment value of $7,000.

The tax consequences of these actions: In the tax year that the transfer occurs, you'll have to report the capital gain of $1,000; 75 per cent of which will be taxable, and you'll have to report the accrued interest on the bonds ($195). Then you'll take a tax deduction for $7,000.

Note: Transfers of assets, as described above, can generally only be made in a self-administered RRSP.

TIPS FOR HOLDING INVESTMENTS IN AN RRSP

1. Consider holding fixed-income, interest-bearing and compounding securities inside your RRSP to avoid the annual accrual rules.
2. Consider holding variable-income securities such as equities outside of your RRSP to maximize use of the 75 per cent income inclusion rate when a disposition occurs. As well, dividends earned outside the RRSP will be taxed advantageously through the dividend tax credit.
3. Move the tax savings you made from the variable-income securities into your RRSP, if you have "room."
4. Accumulations must be withdrawn from an RRSP by the end of the year in which you turn age 71.

CHAPTER 38 Spousal RRSPs

This topic warrants a separate discussion because contributions to a spousal RRSP are often missed or misunderstood. Especially now that common-law unions fall under the same rules as those for legally married couples, opportunities for income splitting in retirement abound with the spousal RRSP rules.

First, let's review the definition of spouse. This is someone of the opposite sex, to whom you are legally married or, in the case of common-law unions, with whom a conjugal relationship has lasted at least 12 months ending in the tax year. However, if the common-law couple has a child, the 12-month cohabitation period is precluded.

This means that if Tom and Joan, a childless couple, lived together from January 1 to December 31 of the tax year in a conjugal relationship, they would qualify as "spouses" for the purposes of the Income Tax Act. If they started living together in November of the tax year, they would not yet meet the "spousal" requirements unless they had a child together. (This includes natural and adoptive children.)

Our previous discussion on RRSP eligibility discussed that "earned income" of the immediately prior year, or prior "contribution room" had to exist in order for the taxpayer to make an RRSP contribution at all. When a taxpayer chooses to make a "Spousal Contribution," it is based on that taxpayer's RRSP room, and that person will also be able to take the deduction for the RRSP contribution.

The spouse, however, becomes the annuitant, or owner of the plan. If the contributions are left in the RRSP for at least three years from the last spousal contribution made, subsequent withdrawals will be taxed in the spouse's hands. Should they be taken out before the three-year period elapses, principal amounts are attributed back to the contributor.

What has been accomplished here is income splitting. If the holding requirements are met, the RRSP contributions will later, upon withdrawal, be taxed in two people's hands instead of one, usually resulting in a lower overall net tax liability. Spouses who transfer the RRSP monies received under this provision to an annuity will be subject to the three year rules. If you transfer the monies to a Registered Retirement Income Fund (RRIF), only amounts withdrawn in excess of minimum withdrawal requirements will be attributed back to the original contributor within the three-year period.

MONEY MANAGEMENT TIP 54

Taxpayers over the age of 71 may still contribute to a Spousal RRSP if their spouse is under age 72.

Sometimes, taxpayers are eligible to contribute amounts to their RRSP over and above their normal RRSP room. This will happen if you receive an eligible retiring allowance from your employer or a refund of premiums due to the death of your spouse, for example. The tax-free rollover allows you to receive such monies on a tax-deferred basis. Generally, these sums can only go into your own RRSP and not your spouse's.

However, 1994 is the last year in which up to $6,000 of periodic pension amounts received by one spouse can be transferred to the RRSP of the other spouse. This is a provision that was available in the period 1989 to 1994. Therefore, March 1, 1995 is the end date for contributions under this rule. Don't miss out!

A person who is over age 71 is prohibited by age from making further RRSP contributions, with the exception of one rule: spousal contributions can be made to your younger spouse's RRSP provided you (the spouse over age 71) still have RRSP contribution room. In this case, the older spouse can still make and claim an RRSP contribution as a deduction.

In the year a spouse dies, a final RRSP contribution may be made to a spousal RRSP and claimed as a deduction on the final return of the deceased. Depending on the amounts involved, this technique can have the effect of reducing the income of the deceased to a level that will allow a Spousal Amount on the return of the surviving spouse, or possibly transfers of credits such as the age amount, disability amount, pension income amount and education/tuition amounts. This final RRSP contribution can be made within 60 days of the end of the year in which the taxpayer died.

Consult with your tax practitioner about the benefits of making a spousal contribution.

> **MONEY MANAGEMENT TIP 55**
>
> Equalize your retirement income by making spousal RRSP contributions during your lifetime. It is better to have these income sources taxed at two lower tax rates than one higher rate.

CHAPTER 39
Revenue Properties

Ownership of revenue properties has many interesting tax consequences. First, there is the claiming of net rental income (or loss) on the tax return. Further tax consequences will result upon conversion of the property from rental to personal use, or from an outright disposition.

These events are the primary basis for separating expenditures for tax purposes. Capital expenditures are those that include the acquisition of the property itself, and any major additions or improvements to it during the time you own it. Such expenditures (with the exception of the value of the land which is not a depreciable asset) are depreciated rather than expensed or written off in full.

Therefore, when you acquire a revenue property, be aware of the following:

1. *Cost of the building*—separated out from the cost of the land—will be added to a Capital Cost Allowance (CCA) statement for the purposes of claiming depreciation. Therefore, have your tax assessment statement or other appraisal at hand when you prepare your tax return. Your legal fees and transfer taxes will be apportioned and capitalized with the cost of the building.

2. *The value of furniture and fixtures* acquired with the building will be separated and placed on the CCA schedule as well. Supporting documentation will be required.

3. Any *major additions or improvements* to the building--such as roofing, carpeting or installation of heating or air conditioning which extend the useful life of the asset—will be added to the capital cost of the building.

4. When new assets or additions/improvements are added to your Capital Cost Allowance Statement, they are grouped according to *asset classifications* set out by Revenue Canada. For example, most buildings would be classed in Class 1 (4 per cent depreciation rate) if acquired after 1978 or Class 6 (10 per cent) if acquired before 1979. Each building valued at $50,000 or more must be reported in a separate Class 1. Furniture and fixtures are usually grouped into Class 8 (20 per cent) and automobiles valued at less than $24,000 in Class l0 (30 per cent).

   In the year of acquisition, there is a special restriction called "the half-year rule." Only one-half of the normal capital cost allowance rates can be claimed on the tax return, subject to the rental loss restriction described below. Therefore, the timing of expenditures on new additions or improvements should be contemplated from the point of view of maximizing your tax benefits.

5. CCA is always taken at the taxpayer's option, with the exception of one rule: *a rental loss cannot be increased or created with a capital cost allowance claim*. Therefore, discuss with your tax preparer when depreciation should be taken, and how much should be taken.

6. CCA is a write-off that can have future tax consequences. If you are claiming CCA to reduce your operating income in a period of time when your assets are appreciating, you may have to pay back the *"recapture"* of CCA previously taken. For example, if your building was acquired for a capital cost of $50,000 and your CCA deduction taken over the years was $10,000, and you turn around and sell it for $75,000, several

consequences come to bear. First, the difference between the undepreciated capital cost of the building ($40,000) and the original costs ($50,000) must be added to your rental income in the year of disposition. The increase in value over the original cost ($25,000) will be treated as a capital gain.

If you did not take enough depreciation during the years you owned an asset—that is the asset depreciated rather than appreciated in value—the difference between the original cost and the disposition proceeds can be claimed as a deduction against rental income in that year. This is called a terminal loss.

Where both a building and its land are deemed disposed of, a terminal loss on the sale of the building is used to reduce any gain on the sale of the land. Separate rules will apply in cases where the taxpayer has died.

Recapture and terminal only occur when all the assets of a class are disposed of.

7. *Operating expenses*—fully deductible against income earned—will include property taxes, interest on mortgage, insurance, utility costs, maintenance and repairs (those activities and expenditures that restore the assets to their original condition), salaries paid to maintenance people or supervisors of the building, accounting expenses, landscaping costs, commissions paid to persons who obtain tenants for you and, in some cases, automobile expenses.

8. *Non-deductible expenses* will include any repayments of principal or any personal expenses. The value of your own labour is never deductible; nor are any expenses pertaining to the cost of the land.

9. *Auto expenses are treated in a special manner.* Taxpayers who own only one rental property may deduct a portion of auto expenses incurred to transport tools and materials to the property. However, the property must be close to the vicinity of your personal residence. If your revenue property is located outside of the city or town in which you live, you will not be able to deduct auto costs, even if you do the repairs for the building yourself.

Auto expenses will be deductible if you own two or more properties and you use the auto to do or supervise repairs, collect rents, show the properties or otherwise manage the properties. Keep all receipts for gas, oil, maintenance and repairs, insurance, license fees, auto club fees, parking and tolls, and a record of distance travelled for the purposes of supervising your property, as well as total distance driven with that vehicle in the year.

10. *Mortgage foreclosures* are subject to special rules. This transaction is really a transfer of the asset back to the creditor. A disposition is considered to have taken place at an amount equal to the unpaid debt plus any legal fees. However, the unpaid debt will not include accrued interest, if it was incurred prior to February 21, 1994. After this date, the proceeds of disposition must take into account the entire debt. This transaction will therefore result in a capital gain or loss computed in the normal manner.

11. When an *operating loss from a rental property occurs* (net operating expenses before capital cost allowance exceed rental income), the loss can be used to offset other income from all sources in the year. Therefore, if you incurred a rental loss of $2,000 and you were in a 50 per cent tax bracket, you would recoup $1,000 in tax savings from this loss.

12. Revenue Canada will restrict *the number of years a rental loss can be claimed* against other income citing that a reasonable expectation of profit does not exist. This gives the department the power to disallow your rental losses unless you can prove that there is a profit motive.

The tax rules surrounding revenue properties are detailed and complex. It would be a good idea to discuss your properties with a tax professional to ensure you are claiming all expenditures to your maximum advantage and that acquisitions and dispositions can be planned with a tax viewpoint.

Revenue properties provide a good way to earn income and capital appreciation. Discuss the tax consequences of the acquisition or conversion of a property to rental use with your tax professional.

CHAPTER 40
The Capital Gains Deduction

To say that the calculations surrounding the Capital Gains Deduction are complex would be an understatement. Since its introduction in May of 1985, it has been tinkered with continuously, until February 22, 1994, when one part of it—the $100,000 deduction on "regular properties"—was eliminated, sort of.

Taxpayers who held capital properties as of February 22, 1994 will have a one-time opportunity to report "accrued gains" on their 1994 income tax returns for the purposes of generating any remaining capital gains deduction they may have. If you acquired capital properties after budget date, there will be no further opportunity to shelter capital gains with the $100,000 capital gains deduction.

Who will this affect? Well, let's go over the list of possible capital properties you might own:
- personal-use properties: a cottage or vacation condo, for example
- listed personal-use properties: a coin or stamp collection, art, jewellery, family heirlooms that have appreciated in value over $1000
- stocks and bonds
- real estate
- eligible capital property

The first step in dealing with this provision in the 1995 tax season is to gather the following information:

1. Capital gains deduction previously used by each person in the family.
2. Find the Cumulative Net Investment Loss (CNIL) balance. CNIL is the excess of investment expenses claimed on your tax return since 1988 over investment income claimed in the same time. If you deducted more in expenses than you claimed in income, your CNIL balance will reduce any available capital gains deduction you may have.
3. Obtain a valuation of your assets as of February 22, 1994.
4. In the case of noncommercial real estate, figure out the following:
   A. How many months have I owned the property after 1971 and before March 1992?
   B. How many months have I owned the property after 1971 and before March 1994?

Divide A by B. This will give you the fraction you'll use to determine your "eligible capital gain" on real property. This calculation is required because noncommercial real estate gains accrued after February 1992 no longer qualified for the capital gains deduction. Therefore, if you acquired real estate after February 1992, you won't need to worry about the capital gains deduction, because you are not entitled to it.

5. If you own only a principle residence, you will also be able to ignore these calculations, as gains on a principle residence can be received on a tax-free basis. However, if you owned a second residence, you will need to find out the following:

    A. If held prior to 1982, what was the value of the properties as at December 31, 1981?

    B. Based on the properties' values on February 22, 1994, which accumulated more in value?

    That property should usually be chosen as the "exempt" principal residence. The other residence would be chosen the "taxable" residence. You may wish to report the accrued gains on your 1994 tax return to use up any capital gains deduction you may have, but whether or not this is beneficial will depend on how long you owned the property prior to March of 1992. (Exclude any "exempt" months in the calculation of your eligible capital gain.)

6. If you currently own shares in a qualifying small business corporation or a qualifying farm property, you will still qualify for the $500,000 Super Exemption. This amount is a cumulative total that must be reduced by any previously claimed $100,000 deduction or other claims previously made under the $500,000 rules.

7. The rules surrounding the election of the capital gains deduction on the 1994 return were sketchy at the time of writing. All taxpayers with accrued gains should seek professional help with this election in the 1995 tax filing season. If you miss the opportunity to elect, you will not be able to go back in retrospect to recover it.

Once you have all the information above at hand, the capital gains election can be calculated.

In some cases there may be a minimum tax liability created by the pre-reporting of the accrued gains. As well, the election may affect other provisions on the tax return including:

- refundable credits such as the Child Tax Benefit and Goods and Services Tax Credit
- provincial net income taxes
- Old Age Security supplements

- medical expenses and charitable donation claims
- any other provisions affected by the size of your net income

COMPUTATION OF CAPITAL GAINS FOR THE PURPOSE OF THE CAPITAL GAINS ELECTION
Complete one calculation for each taxable property.
Based on February 22, 1994 budget proposals

Capital Gains Deduction Available $_____(1) CNIL Balance $_____(2)
Identification of Property _____ Date Acquired _____

To determine Capital Gain or Loss on Properties actually sold before February 22, 1994:
Go to Schedule 3, T657 and T936 and compute in normal manner.

I. Calculation of Accrued Gain to February 22, 1994

FMV of your asset as at February 22, 1994 $_____ a
ACB $_____ b
CAPITAL GAIN $_____ c

II. Determination of Deemed Proceeds of Disposition if Accrued Gains exceed CGD Room: (If this does not apply go to Part III below)

(1) Accrued Gain (amount c above)   _____ d
(2) Capital Gains Deduction room (1) above   _____ e
    Lesser of (d) and (e)   _____ f
(3) ACB (b) above _____ + (f) _____ = _____ g
(4) CNIL Adjustment:* CNIL (2) above _____ x 4/3 _____ h
(5) Proceeds of Disposition (g) + (h)   _____ i
    Transfer to line (k), Part IV below.

III. Determination of Accrued Capital Gain for February 22, 1994 Election Purposes

(1) Choose an amount between ACB (b) above _____ &
    Fair Market Value as at February 22, 1994 (a) above _____ _____ j
    Transfer to line (k), Part IV below.

IV. Determination of Accrued Capital Gain for February 22, 1994 Election Purposes

Proceeds of Disposition   less   Adjusted Cost Base   =   Gain for Election
(Choose (i) or (j) above)   (Choose (b) above)   (Losses not used)
_____(k)   _____(l)   _____(m)

Take 3/4 of amount (m) to line 1 of T657. Take full amount of line (m) to Schedule 3.
If actual disposition occurs after February 22, 1994, complete Part V below:

V. Determination of Capital Gain or Loss on Actual Disposition Occurring after Feb. 22, 1994

Actual Proceeds of   less   Amended ACB   =   Capital Gain or Loss
Disposition   Amount (k) above
_____   _____   _____(n)

Use Form T664 to make your Capital Gains Election.

* Note: A similar adjustment may be made for losses claimed on your tax returns.

MONEY MANAGEMENT TIP 56

A new adjusted cost base will be created by pre-reporting of accrued capital gains, so that future capital gains on actual disposition are reduced by any amounts pre-reported. If your asset actually goes down in value from the pre-reported amount, capital losses must be increased by any previously reported gains.

LIFE CYCLES: BUILDING YOUR FINANCIAL PYRAMID

CHAPTER 41
Early Childhood: Birth to Age 12

Money management begins with the first dollar your child receives. This could be a gift upon his or her arrival in this world. It could be money received as gifts throughout childhood. Soon it might be earnings from a paper route, babysitting or other part-time job.

> **MONEY MANAGEMENT TIP 57**
>
> Start a money management plan with the very first dollar your child receives in his or her own right.

While your child is very young, you must save and produce for that child, until he or she is old enough to do so. But along the way, good money management skills can be acquired by setting the right example. Start saving money for your child immediately. Give your child the opportunity to "pull ahead" from a financial point of view.

Your child will be proud to accompany you to the local financial institution as you save money for his or her future. This should begin with the opening of two accounts:

   Account No. 1: Child Tax Benefits Account
   Account No. 2: Birthday and other gifts

Account No. 1. Deposit all Child Tax Benefits received for your child in that separate "untainted" account. Any resulting interest earnings from the principal accumulated in this account, or subsequent investments to which you might move the accumulated capital to, will be taxed in the child's hands. This account is an excellent start to an "education fund" for your child. It is totally self-administered. You decide how and where to invest the capital accumulations.

Once your accumulations are $500 or more, you should consider moving the money out of the low-yield savings account and into another type of investment. This could be a fixed-income investment such as a Guaranteed Income Certificate or a bond. Check minimum investment levels with your financial institution.

It would likely be best to have your child earn interest or dividends out of this source, as the resulting earnings will be tax sheltered.

Account No. 2. Deposit all gifts of money to the Birthday/Gift account. Technically interest earned on this account must be divided up and reported by the adult who gave the child the money. Therefore, if you give your child money for his or her birthday, you will have to report the initial interest earned until the child reaches age 18. However, reinvestment of interest earnings or "second generation" earnings will be taxed back in the child's hands.

The same rule holds true if a grandparent gives money to the child. The grandparent must report the interest earnings until the child reaches age 18. These attribution rules will hold true for both dividend and interest earnings, but not for capital gains generated by the investment.

Therefore, parents may wish to gift the child "birthday stocks" or "birthday mutual funds." Resulting capital gains will be taxed in the child's hands. You may wish to move the required minimum capital accumulations out of Account No. 2 and into an equity investment as soon as possible, or parents or grandparents may wish to make a direct investment into an equity for these purposes.

MONEY MANAGEMENT TIP 58

Monies given to a child by a non-resident grandparent are not subject to the attribution rules. Therefore if a European or Asian-resident grandparent gives a gift of, let's say, $5,000 to a child, resulting investment earnings will be taxed in the child's hands.

CHAPTER 42
Your Child's Education Fund

It is never too soon to start an education fund for your child, even if having a family is still in the planning stage. Whether your children go on to university or college, or other formal training institution, an education is a major investment that will pay dividends over and over again in the future.

> **MONEY MANAGEMENT TIP 59**
> Begin your child's education fund as soon as possible.

HOW MUCH DO YOU NEED?

Your window of opportunity for multiplying your disposable dollars in an education fund is generally 18 years, if you begin when your child is born.

If your child goes to university for four years, at an average cost of $7,500 a year (including tuition, books, student fees and residence), you will need $30,000 per child, in today's after-tax dollars, to finance their education costs.

However, at an average inflation rate of 4 per cent, the purchasing power of that fund would be reduced roughly by half in 18 years.

There are a couple of ways to approach this potential mega-problem.

1. *Move your tax savings into an education fund.* Deposit Child Tax Benefits received in the name of the child (as previously discussed). Use tax refunds from RRSP deposits or preferential tax treatment on dividends or capital gains to deposit into the education fund. If you can accumulate new money in a lump sum of $1,000 at the end of each year, and invest it at an average rate of 8 per cent, you'll have accumulated a pre-tax portfolio of $37, 450. Your $1,000 in new money results from a saving of only $2.75 per day. Therefore, if you have two children, save $5.50 a day; three children $8.25 a day and so on.

2. *Have your children help out and help themselves.* To account for tax and inflation erosion, tell your children that they are responsible for half of

the bill and have them save a loonie a day from gifts or part-time jobs to finance their education.

Remember, if you invest the money in the lower-income earner's hands, it will grow on a tax-free or tax-sheltered basis over the rates paid by the higher-income earner. Your child will also have a stake in his or her education.

Your own attitude towards saving and investing money will have a huge influence on your child or grandchild. Teach your child to save (see Chapter 14).

The savings for the education fund can take place in a Registered Education Savings Plan (RESP), or also outside of a "registered plan."

REGISTERED EDUCATION SAVINGS PLANS

Parents and grandparents are often particularly concerned about saving for a child's future education and can be foiled in their savings attempts by high tax rates. Some set up a Registered Education Savings Plan for that purpose. RESPs are a way to split income off to the child and shelter interest earnings from tax while the education fund grows.

The way the plan works is that you would contribute your after-tax dollars to the RESP. You do not receive a tax deduction for this. However, while the principal accumulates interest earnings, it is not taxed back to you. The earnings accumulate tax-free until the child starts to receive funds from the plan. At that point only the interest—not the principal—becomes subject to tax, but in the child's hands. Presumably the child will be in a low tax bracket while going to school, so the minimum amount of tax—if any—will be paid on the accumulations.

The principle contributions are usually returned to the contributor. However, the earnings cannot be. They must be paid out as a "scholarship."

Contributions to RESPs have been limited to $1,500 annually since February 20, 1990. The overall maximum contribution limit is $31,500 for each beneficiary. The plans must terminate in 25 years, and education benefits can only be paid to full-time students at designated post-secondary educational institutes. Because of these restrictions, parents and grandparents should carefully consider all the consequences of making this investment. New plans and features emerge annually.

INSIDE OR OUTSIDE A RESP?

Remember, Account No. 1 as described in Chapter 41, containing any Child Tax Benefit payments received, should be initiated first by the parents.

These payments are dependent upon the size of your family net income. Higher-income earners will have no choice but to look for other tax-deferred savings mechanisms if they don't qualify to receive these benefits. At first glance, the choice appears to be between tax-sheltered compounding within a RESP and annually taxable returns of interest earnings outside of a RESP. However, there are several ways this might be dealt with, including making equity investments whose capital gains returns are only taxed upon disposition. Discuss these options with your financial advisor.

CHAPTER 43: Wealth-Producing Teenagers

Jason, a 19-year-old college junior, living in Winnipeg, bought his first home when he was 18 years old. He had accumulated his down payment of $30,000 on his $50,000 row house in the five-year period from age 13 to 18. Every year Jason worked diligently, while keeping up his grades at school. He never frittered away his money. Here's how he saved:

1. *Age 13 to 15:*

Babysitting every morning and after school for a neighbour	$50.00 a week
Paper route	$20.00 a week
Cut grass/snowshovelling	$20.00 a week
Total (assumes no expenses):	$300 a month or $3,600 a year

2. *Age 16 to 18:*

Weekend job 16 hours/week	$96.00 a week
Babysitting every morning and after school	$50.00 a week
Paper route	$20.00 a week
Yard work	$20.00 a week
Total	$744 a month or $8,928 a year

3. *Total gross earnings:*

Age 13 to 15:	$10,800
Age 16 to 18:	$26,784*
Total gross earnings (before investment earnings and taxes):	$37,584

*Note that taxes would be about $700 each year if no expenses were claimed, if Jason did not maximize his RRSP room, and interest income was about $300.

Jason's parents, as a reward for his diligence, gave him a tax-free gift of $20,000 on his 18th birthday, which he used for the investment in the property. Proudly, he moved into his new, clear title principal residence. To help pay for operating costs such as taxes and utilities, Jason took in a boarder.** Jason's part-time job continued to help finance his education costs. Two years later, Jason sold his home for $58,000 and made his first tax-exempt capital gain—not a bad tax-free investment for a young man.

While such a series of transactions may be more difficult in more expensive cities such as Toronto or Vancouver, this story does illustrate the potential capital accumulation a diligent young person might have while living at home in a virtually tax-free and cost-sheltered environment—a great alternative to idling around the corner store!

Jason could have made a critical error when he turned 16. He could have bought a depreciating asset, such as a new car. The purchase of a car can only be a good investment if it helps the child make more money, at a part-time job or to get to school, for example. Most cars, however, are a bottomless, depreciating pit eating up potential investment capital, especially if a youth is the only one in his group of friends who has "wheels." If a vehicle is a must, sit down and draw up a budget for gas, oil, maintenance, insurance and license fees. Take a good hard look at resale values of new cars, only a month or two after they are driven off the lot. Then look at the alternatives: car pooling, bussing and using a family car are cheaper alternatives, if not the most convenient or prestigious. And if your child is the car pool driver, insist that he or she work out cost-sharing arrangements with friends.

Between the ages of 13 and 18, your child may have the opportunity to work at his or her first job and formulate a picture of the future. With your guidance, your teenagers will develop and grow into frugal and productive adults who can accumulate large sums of capital in their own right.

This is the time that your child will enter the capital marketplace for the first time, and learn of the responsibility that comes with making

---
** Not taxable, as there is no profit motive.

sound investment decisions. Any entrepreneurial bank manager will recognize this huge opportunity to earn a "client for life." He or she should jump at the opportunity of introducing your child to the fascinating new world of personal money management and the potential new business with investments in GICs and RRSPs, and mortgage or consumer loan possibilities.

The more your child knows about the investment possibilities available, the more goal oriented he or she will be. Draw up a series of objectives with your teenagers as soon as they start accumulating money. Ideas for such objectives might include the following:

TEN-POINT FINANCIAL STARTER PLAN FOR TEENAGERS

1. *Shop around for a financial institution for your child.* Treat this as the major event it is. Starting a relationship with a financial institution is akin to a new relationship with a doctor or lawyer. You might begin with the same branch the family traditionally deals with. But by using the "three-quote method" outlined in Part 1, look specifically for a branch that is interested enough in this potentially long-term relationship with your child to take the time to do the following:
   - meet the manager of the branch
   - have a "starter account" for young people without expensive service charges
   - explain simple investment options, both fixed and variable rate
   - identify minimum investment amounts required to make such investments
   - explain the responsibilities surrounding the ownership of a banking card

2. *Hand over the management of Account No. 2 to your child.* (Do this while your child is still in "listening mode," which ends the day before he or she turns 14, if your household resembles ours at all!) This is the account that housed birthday money and other gifts. Explain that these monies should be kept in a separate account because their initial earnings are attributed back to the donor. However, second-generation earnings created from the reinvestment of interest are taxed in the hands of the child. Therefore, all the monies become principal of the child once the initial tax is paid. Investment decisions can now be made together with the parent—a good way to gain valuable investment experience.

3. *Hang onto the management of Account No. 1—the Education Fund.* This is the account that housed any Child Tax Benefit monies. If you do not

qualify for the CTB by virtue of your high net family income, gift the child capital assets instead. (The attribution rules do not extend to capital gains-producing investments.) Let your child know about the fund, and how much of the education expense you expect that child to be responsible for. While many parents pay their child's education costs outright, both students and parents have later commented that an education is more highly valued if the child must also make contributions to it. Books and living expenses are not tax deductible—tuition is. You might discuss several financing alternatives with your child such as:

- parents will pay half of the tuition and half of the living costs
- parents will pay all of the tuition and none of the books or living costs
- parents will pay none of the expenses but give the child the education fund to use as a future down payment on a house or car upon graduation

Your child needs to know about these plans well before his or her 18th birthday to start preparing for the expensive post-secondary education years.

4. *If the child has any self-employment earnings, open a separate account.* This could include earnings from a paper route or child care. Business earnings can be offset with out-of-pocket expenses that should be paid for through the business account. A separate business account will make tax filing easier. A young entrepreneur needs to be able to write cheques and keep a cash flow balance, so teach your child these skills.

5. *Begin a forced savings plan.* If the young adult works as an employee—perhaps in your business—deposit those earnings directly into a Canada Savings Bond purchased through a payroll savings plan, or another bank account if such a plan is not available.

6. *Teach your child to prepare a bank reconciliation*, so that bank charges can be tracked. Such services charges are tax deductible in the business account.

7. *File a tax return every year for your working child.* From a tax point of view, your teenager should begin filing a tax return as soon as she or he has their first job—even if the child is not taxable. The reason for this is to create "unused RRSP contribution room" that can be carried forward and used to offset taxable income in the future. Unused contribution room of one year can be carried forward seven years. Therefore, if your child earned $800 in the year babysitting for a neighbour, 18 per cent of this, or $144, becomes qualifying contribution room that can be accumulated for future use.

8. *Consider making RRSP contributions for your child.* Your teenager must have "earned income" before an RRSP contribution can be made. Your child may contribute to an RRSP but not take the deduction if he or she is not taxable. These contributed but undeducted contributions can be carried forward and claimed on the tax return in a future year when the child's earnings are in a higher bracket and the tax deduction is needed. In the meantime, the fund accumulates tax-sheltered earnings.

9. *Can you overcontribute to a child's RRSP?* For adults (those over 18), an overcontribution limit of up to $8,000 can be made to an RRSP without incurring a penalty. The idea is to make the overcontribution and carry it forward to a year in which the required taxable income warrants a deduction. However, this option is specifically prohibited for children under 18. In fact, minors may not contribute to an RRSP in excess of contribution room at all. Therefore, any savings over and above this should be invested in interest, dividend and capital gains-bearing investments outside of the RRSP.

10. *Put your child to work, tax free.* Your child will not be taxable unless total taxable income exceeds $6,456, the basic personal amount. Canada Pension Plan premiums will not be payable until the month in which the child turns 18; however, unemployment insurance premiums will be payable if certain amounts of earnings or hours are worked each week. And remember, earned income will qualify to create RRSP room.

    You can employ your child in your own business and pay that child a wage that is tax deductible to you and reportable to him or her. The amounts paid must be reasonable in relation to the work that is actually done and would be paid to a stranger doing the same task. Office cleaning, packing, delivery of advertising flyers, client service or other tasks, depending on the type of business you own, are excellent ways to legally split income within the family. Keep time cards or other records of work time and issue T4 slips in the usual manner.

> **MONEY MANAGEMENT TIP 60**
>
> Your teenager, age 13 to 19, is in a very important stage of life for starting a money-management plan. Don't miss this important opportunity to take advantage of income splitting, capital accumulation and compounding time. Let time work wonders for your child.

CHAPTER 44
The Power Learning Years

In a global economy, lifelong learning will be the key to success in the future. Most of us can expect to be training and retraining throughout our careers. However, it is those years between age 18 and 25 that we can expect to use as "Power Learning" years.

Whether you spend this time at university, college or in a trade or business apprenticeship, the need for budgeting of time and money will be critical.

If you and your parents have worked hard, your basic education costs may already be covered with previous savings. If not, you'll each have to make decisions that result in meeting your objectives with the least amount of hardship.

Post-secondary education can be a bit of a culture shock. While you were nurtured along through to high school, you are really responsible for what you make of your educational opportunities after this. You must be self-motivated and disciplined, and be extremely competitive in some fields. The pressures can be enormous.

That is why it is most important not to have to worry about your financial affairs in this time. *An education is an investment in yourself.* If you spend your time wisely, it will pay off handsomely later when you get the job you want or start the business that will lead to your financial independence. In the meantime, here are some typical income sources, deductions and credits a student might run into during the Power Learning Years.

YOUR INCOME FOR TAX PURPOSES

Income Source	Tax Status	Action Required
Employment Income	Fully taxable.	Reduce total income with RRSP contributions. Transfer to the supporting person education/tuition credits.
Research Grants	Net grants taxable.	Reduce grants with out-of-pocket expenses.
Scholarships and Bursaries	Taxable, with exemption.	Reduce by $500 tax exemption.

Income Source	Tax Status	Action Required
Fellowships	Taxable, with exemption if purpose is to further individual pursuit of a degree.	Reduce by $500 tax exemption.
RESP Income	Interest earnings fully taxable when paid to student as "scholarship."	Report as "Other Income."

YOUR SPECIAL TAX DEDUCTIONS AND CREDITS

Deduction/Credit	Tax Status	Action Required
GST Credit	Up to $199 annually at time of writing.	File a tax return starting at age 19 to recoup this credit for the individual.
Child Tax Benefit	Amounts vary with number of children, marital status and family income.	File a tax return to receive these monthly benefits if you are supporting a child.
RRSPs	Contributions possible if you have "room."	Save for use against future employment income unless a tuition/education transfer can be created for supporting persons.
Child Care Expenses	Up to $5,000 for children under 7 or $3,000 children age 7 to 14. Special rules for disabled children.	Claimable by student or by spouse who may be the higher income earner. In latter case, claim is restricted to $150 for children under 7 and $90 a week for those age 7 to 14.
Moving Expenses	Incurred to earn income or take scholarships/ bursaries or start new job or business.	Claim cost of move and temporary living accommodations (up to 15 days).
Spousal Amount	Up to $5,380 can be claimed.	Includes common-law unions. You may be claimable by spouse if your income is less than $5,918. If both of you are students, you might transfer tuition/education amounts to parents or grandparents.
Equivalent-to-Spouse	Up to $5,380 for single parents or singles who support dependent parents or grandparents	Based on dependant's net income. Must be residing with dependant in a dwelling maintained by you.

Income Source	Tax Status	Action Required
Foreign Universities	Tuition fees paid will qualify for a tax credit.	Must attend for 13 consecutive weeks in a program leading to degree.
Tuition Fees	Qualify for tax credit if amounts paid exceed $100.	Claimable for amounts paid for sessions in calendar year only. No upper dollar maximum. Does not include costs of books or student activity fees.
Education Credit	$80 monthly credit.	For full-time attendance at a post-secondary institution in courses lasting at least 3 weeks with at least 10 hours a week of study time.
Tuition/Education Transfer	Up to $4,000.	To supporting parent, spouse or grandparent if you are not taxable.
Provincial Tax Credits	Vary with province of residence.	Usually only available to those age 18 or over. Can include sales tax, cost of living, property tax credits.
Cost of Books	Not deductible with exception.	Cost of books which are an integral part of correspondence courses will be deductible as part of all-inclusive fees.
Student Loans	Interest costs are not deductible.	Tax refunds can be garnisheed if you fail to repay loan.

MONEY MANAGEMENT TIP 61

Students: Have fun, but resist the temptation to party hearty. Stick to a capital accumulation plan. Partying will not only make studying much more difficult, but it will also eat up much of your spare change. If you can, you should still try to stick to a capital accumulation plan of some kind throughout your full-time study period. Remember, in your youth you have compounding time on your side. You will have a better lifestyle later if you remember to start saving now. Don't forget to file a tax return.

WHAT A DIFFERENCE STARTING EARLY CAN MAKE
**Investment of $1,000 at an annual compounding rate of 10%;
first deposit is immediate and before tax**

A. Student invests $1,000 a year for 10 years, starting at age 20, then leaves the balance on deposit		B. Post-study investment at $1,000 a year, starting at age 30	
Age	Accumulations	Age	Accumulations
20	$ 1,000	20	Nil
30	17,531	30	$ 1,000
40	45,470	40	17,531
50	117,939	50	63,002
Total Capital Invested: $10,000		Total Capital Invested: $20,000	

Even though Student A invested only half as much capital, he or she ends up with over twice as much at the end of a 40-year period than Student B. It pays to save first, party later.

Remember that a $1,000 capital investment results from saving only $2.74 a day. Actions required: stop smoking, eat a bagged lunch, car pool, buy used books, live at home, park your car.

Why is this important? Well, perhaps at little later in life, you will assume a mortgage. The question you will be asking yourself at that time will be "Do I pay off my mortgage or contribute to my RRSP?" If you contribute early in life to your RRSP, you can, if you want to, coast along letting compounding and time work together to multiply your retirement savings within the RRSP. In the meantime, you can sock away more money towards your non-deductible mortgage payments in the 25-year period between age 30 and 55, and perhaps cut both your amortization period and your interest payments. (Remember, though, that the RRSP contributions you make will create "new money" through tax savings, which is particularly important as your marginal tax rates increase. See Chapter 49.)

Student B would have a much tougher time managing both the RRSP fund and the mortgage effort if he or she foolishly spent disposable dollars in the first 10 years.

The first 12 years of adulthood (ages 18 to 30) are therefore critical in the firm establishment of your lifetime financial plan.

CHAPTER 45
Family Mode

In the 20-year period from age 20 to 40, you'll be making so many first-time decisions that you can only hope that the thinking skills you have acquired in your first 20 years of formal schooling will give you the common sense to make adequate judgment calls. The resulting experiences you will encounter will give you that aura of wisdom surrounding some of the 45-year-olds you know today!

Let's chart some of these "firsts" and what you should watch out for from a money management viewpoint.

A NEW PARTNER

There is tremendous optimism and delight in the union of two people who have decided to build a family together. When you begin a relationship with another person, your financial affairs will change completely. Each of you will want to revisit the construction of your net worth statement, cash flow statement, and family objectives and budgets, as discussed in Part 1. Your union will be a partnership in many different ways. Your financial affairs may strengthen, as the financial forces and productive power of two join to work towards one goal. However, sometimes those goals, which may begin in unison, drift apart.

A PRENUPTIAL OR SPOUSAL AGREEMENT

Usually a commitment to marriage or other long-term conjugal relationship is made with the notion that love will conquer all. "For better, for worse" and "Till death do us part" are parts of the marriage vows that are taken by many couples. Unfortunately, statistics tell us that about 50 per cent of the time, conjugal relationships will end in failure, often with severe emotional and financial consequences.

Throughout this book, we have attempted to give you ideas to help you travel along the road to financial independence. We have examined risk factors and hedges against loss. Now, in looking at one of the most important decisions of your life—who will you choose to be your lifelong partner—

we must challenge you. Would you invest your time and money in any venture that has a 50 per cent risk factor? What precautions would you take if you did? These are hard questions when you relate them to emotional matters.

However, if you know of someone who has been through a relationship failure, you might have been shocked at how two people, who once loved each other enough to make an intimate commitment to each other, can treat each other and their families with such malice when things go wrong.

> **MONEY MANAGEMENT TIP 62**
> Consider a prenuptial agreement before you begin a conjugal relationship.

In many cases, one spouse—often (but not always) the woman who is perhaps unskilled and absent from the labour force—is left financially destitute and with full financial responsibility for the raising of the children. Perhaps she thought she'd always be looked after. Perhaps she felt secure. She finds she was wrong.

If you face the statistical odds before you commit to marriage, legal or common law, you will take off the rose-coloured glasses long enough to consider a prenuptial or spousal agreement. Think about it. You would probably not enter a business relationship of such a proposed length and magnitude without one, particularly not if you knew up front this "investment" had a 50 per cent chance of failure.

This agreement should clearly spell out which assets are brought into the marriage by each partner. It might stipulate that future wealth should be allocated in accordance with original capital invested and the active participation of wealth creation in the time the partners were together*. It might also outline who is responsible when one partner incurs debt without the approval of the other. Most importantly, the agreement should set out the clear and legal responsibility each parent has for the care and maintenance of the children they decide to have together. A child should not suffer because his or her parents' union dissolves.

Would it hold up in court? Discuss the following with your legal representative: structuring inheritances; who is to be responsible for paying child support; business interests; child custody issues; interprovincial and international enforcement issues.

Separation and divorce is a very expensive process. Legal fees to obtain a separation or divorce are also not tax deductible. Make sure you can keep your head above water when the unexpected happens to you.

---

* In most provinces equal possession of the matrimonial home is law.

A NEW SET OF OBJECTIVES

You may be thinking of starting a family and perhaps buying a home. Your lifestyle will certainly change as you prepare for the responsibilities of maintaining your property and nurturing your family. Many young couples use the first few years of their relationship to capitalize on their joint earning power. They acquire consumer items they'll need when they start a family in view that one income will drop off, at least temporarily. Together, you might design your financial objectives to encompass the following objectives:

Financial Objectives for Our New Partnership

1. Try to save one-half of each paycheque every pay period.
2. At a minimum, try to save $100 every pay period.
3. Establish an emergency fund of four months' earnings.
4. Invest the maximum in an RRSP.
5. Use the Spousal RRSP provisions to equalize retirement pension savings. (The chart below illustrates why it is so important to consider your RRSP investment first.)
6. Discuss strategy for investments outside an RRSP.
   • Conservative: GICs, bonds, debentures, preferred shares, etc.
   • Moderate Risk: Equities, certain mutual funds, real estate, etc.
   • Aggressive: Tax shelters, art, precious metals, certain mutual funds, equities, real estate
7. Discuss insurance needs (see Chapter 46).
8. Discuss the preparation of a will.
9. Plan for your home: Will you buy, rent or live at home? (See Chapter 47.) Establish a mortgage savings fund. Sock away as much money as you can before you commit yourself to a mortgage. The higher the down payment, the more choices you will have. Once you begin to contemplate a purchase, shop around—a lot. Location is vital; so are mortgage rates and terms. You may wish to play it safe and budget your house payments on one income, not two. This will force you to buy a home you can afford, taking into account several unforeseen events that you may not plan on when you are making the decision to buy. (such as surprise pregnancies, illness, job loss, unexpected moves, hikes in interest rates at mortgage renewal time, etc.) Consider using the second income, if there is one, to pay down this non-deductible debt, either through a bigger down payment, increased periodic payments or annual principal pay-downs. (See Chapter 47.)

10. Set up an education fund and start saving now for your children's future.
11. Credit card use: Discuss when and how to use. Plan for short-term use only. Should cards be jointly or individually held?
12. Discuss your "debt elimination strategies" *before* you incur any debt. Make sure you both know who is responsible for debt incurred, and how it will be handled.

WHAT A DIFFERENCE TAX SHELTERING CAN MAKE
Investment of $1,000 each year at an annual compounding rate of 10%; first deposit is made immediately

Years	Value of an investment outside an RRSP. Principal in after-tax dollars: $720.* Assuming a 28% tax rate. (7.2% after-tax rate of return.)	Value of an investment inside an RRSP. Principal in pre-tax dollars: $1,000. (No taxable withdrawal in the period.)
10	$ 10,765	$ 17,531
20	32,342	63,003
30	75,585	180,943
40	162,256	486,852
50	335,964	1,280,299

*We have assumed the original $1,000 principal used for investment was taxed at 28 per cent to leave only $720 net to invest. The $720 will earn interest of 10 per cent, but this is taxed annually. This means that for every dollar earned, 28 cents is taken away for tax purposes, leaving an after-tax rate of return of only 7.2 per cent.

Difference of investing inside rather than outside an RRSP: at first glance $944,335. But remember your RRSP withdrawals will be taxable later. If we assume the money is pulled out at a 28 per cent tax rate over a period of time, and earns no more, you'll have $921,851 after tax, leaving you $585,851 richer at retirement.

A NEW TAX STATUS

When you live together with someone, new tax consequences arise. First of all, you will be considered "single" if you live common law with someone of the opposite sex for less than a 12-month period ending on December 31, unless you *previously* live together for a 12-month period. Therefore, if you and your girlfriend/boyfriend move in together in July and by October find it's not working, and so you separate, you will be considered "single" for tax purposes for the whole year. If you live together for at least a 12-month period ending in the tax year, you will be considered to be "spouses" for the purposes of filing a tax return.

However, if you and your friend started living together at any time in the year, and continue to live together at year end, and you have a natural or adoptive child together, you will be considered to be "spouses" for the purposes of the Income Tax Act, and all the same provisions will apply to you as to married couples for the entire tax year.

Depending on the size of your net family income, several new provisions will apply to you if your marital status changes:
- You may be eligible for the Spousal Amount if your spouse's income is under $5,918 in 1994.
- You may be eligible to transfer one or several of the following tax credits to your return:
    i) the $1,000 pension income amount
    ii) the Age Amount
    iii) the Disability Amount
    iv) the Tuition/Education Amount
- You'll be able to make a Spousal RRSP contribution (described above).
- You may be able to group and claim medical expenses on either return, whichever is more beneficial to your household.
- You may be able to group and claim charitable donations to your best advantage.
- You may be able to group and claim political contributions to your best advantage.
- You may be able to split up the moving expenses (if at least 40 km closer to a new place of work, school or business) to your best advantage.
- You may qualify for an additional Goods and Services Tax Credit.
- You may qualify for a Child Tax Benefit.
- You may be able to transfer dividends from your spouse.
- There may be special provincial tax credits for your new dependants.
- You may be able to claim child care expenses under certain conditions.
- Changes may be required to adjust the level of tax deducted at source at your employment to reflect your new personal situation.
- As you combine financial resources, new tax consequences will arise on your investment diversification. Be aware of the attribution rules, particularly for family residences (see Chapter 31).

MONEY MANAGEMENT TIP 63
Review your tax status as soon as you begin a conjugal relationship with someone of the opposite sex.

CHAPTER 46
Essential Financial Protection for Young Families

When your family is young and your energy level is high, and your job is secure, it is difficult to image that your fortunes will do anything but rise. But imagine these events for a moment:

1. Young mother of two children is stricken with disease and cannot look after her children.
2. Father, age 38, is diagnosed with cancer and passes away within six months.
3. Parents, age 36 and 34, lose the business they've built up for 10 years.
4. Mother, age 32, is disabled permanently and cannot work.
5. Unskilled mother, age 39, learns that her husband is leaving her and that the family resources are depleted.
6. Eighteen-year-old father copes with university and a young child.

In a nutshell, this is life. Even if you think everything is great today, you will never know when you'll hit a curve in the road. In this decade, there can be no excuse for "blind trust." You must prepare yourself for difficult times, even if your conjugal relationship, your job or business and personal health are great today. It's when things go wrong that you will really need those "soft assets"—a good marriage, good health and good support systems—to pull you through.

There are several concrete things you can do to proactively practice "disaster management":

1. Set up an emergency fund to pull you through on a short-term basis: one to four months (see Parts 1 and 2 for details).
2. Buy the right amount and type of insurance.
3. Consider a Prenuptial or Spousal Agreement (see Chapter 45).

THE RIGHT AMOUNT OF INSURANCE

In Part 1 of this book, we listed the different types of risks your family might run into, and spoke of the importance of adequate insurance protection.

Which of these risks should be covered by insurance and which should be managed in other ways?

First of all, you must ask yourself, how much risk can you assume without purchasing additional or outside insurance? How much money could you raise quickly if you had to? Would this cover small emergencies?

Next, think about the income-producing assets that must be insured. You can usually make this decision by examining what protection is "essential," "nice, if the price is right" or "strictly optional." Always think about these three factors while you are listening to a presentation by an insurance agent. Then know what the different options are—although this may take some study on your part.

Essential insurance will cover the assets you would not be able to replace or handle out of your current income if disaster strikes. Losses of this magnitude could bring on severe hardship or even bankruptcy. In this category are 1. death of the main breadwinners; 2. disability of the main breadwinners; and 3. loss of source of income.

LIFE INSURANCE

Should you die prematurely, your life insurance policy proceeds would have to adequately protect your family's needs and lifestyle. They may also need to cover any tax liability that may arise due to the deemed disposition of your assets at fair market value at the time of your demise, should other assets not be sufficient to offset the liability.

You may wish for your life insurance policy to pay off your mortgage. It may well be cheaper for you to increase the amount of your life insurance rather than take mortgage insurance from your lender, so compare the rates.

You may wish for your life insurance policy proceeds to be large enough to generate required annual income from the reinvestment of the benefit paid. Life insurance policy proceeds, by the way, are not taxable to the recipient, but their resulting earnings are.

There are three main types of life insurance you can buy: 1. term or renewable insurance; 2. permanent or whole life insurance; and 3. universal life.

Term insurance simply insures a life for the term of the policy. You'll often hear agents refer to this as a "rental" policy—like renting a house, you have all the benefits of home ownership but no equity. A term policy can give you a lot of insurance coverage when you need it most (i.e., when you have many and/or young dependants) for a lower cost. It can also be very important for those who own a small business (i.e., for "keyman" insurance coverage of outstanding debts at your demise, and partnership relations).

The only time the policy pays out is if the insured dies. There is no savings component. If the insured outlives the term of the policy, he or she gets nothing. Premiums have paid only for the insurance protection. You are, therefore, at risk if your policy is not "guaranteed renewable"; that is, renewable in the future without having to repeat a medical examination. Term insurance premiums are usually much lower than those of whole life insurance. However, the older you are, the more expensive these premiums will be. The premiums will usually increase at the end of a term and the policy will usually be cancelled at age 75. There are, however, "Term to 100" policies available, which do feature endowment (payout of face value) when you reach age 100.

A whole life insurance policy will insure your life for a level premium and give you a variety of other "bells and whistles" such as cash values, rights to borrow against or withdraw cash values, a variety of premium payment options and the option to have a paid-up policy at a certain time. This is generally based on dividend returns.

Dividends are "paid" to policyholders as a return emerges in the company's profit levels due to changes in mortality rates, market conditions and other variables. There are three ways to have dividends paid:

- as cash or a credit used to lower premiums or in cash (these amounts are not taxable)
- on an accumulating basis, in which case some tax exposure may result under the annual interest accrual rules, if earnings exceed the policy's adjusted cost base
- on an accumulating basis, but at the policyholder's option, to be used to buy more insurance. This last option is a good way to beat inflationary forces and the possibility of uninsurability due to disability.

For example, *a combination whole life plus term policy* will allow you to have the permanence of a whole life paid-up policy with the lower costs of a term policy. In other words, a person who needs insurance but doesn't have the resources to pay for whole life can benefit with a combination term and whole life policy.

A *whole life with dividend policy* is very expensive, but will generate higher returns in its savings feature. Aggressive policyholders can pay such policies off in eight to 10 years. The primary benefit is that after paying up, you will continue to benefit from tax-deferred and increasing dividends and cash values.

Whole life with no dividend policies are less expensive because there are no dividends payable, but they can be paid up at an earlier date, if desired.

A *universal policy* offers the policyholder a variety of flexible options including premium payment options, choice of investment funds, and a choice of death benefits. Fund values will, of course, vary with the activities of the marketplace and will not always be guaranteed. Certain universal policies will guarantee funds incorporated into them.

Because of the different options and costs, the key to acquiring the best insurance policy for your needs lies with the skill of your insurance representative. Like the purchase of any other assets, a thorough needs analysis should be performed both by the salesperson and the client, while the education process in terms of product features is properly detailed. Your representative must understand your needs and budget to do the best job for you. Be sure you have thought about the following in advance:

1. How much protection do I need, and why?
2. For how long will I need protection?
3. Will I need this protection at retirement?
4. Will I want retirement benefits from my insurance policy?
5. What are the costs of such benefits (in projected dollars):
   a. as paid into the policy?
   b. as invested outside the policy?
6. Are cash flow requirements for taxes addressed if I die?
7. Have I taken the effects of inflation into account?
8. Will there be a disability waiver to carry on the premiums if I become disabled?

Most insurance representatives I have met are knowledgeable in their product lines as well as in tax and money management matters; sincere about helping me make the best decision for my specific needs; and available to answer all of my questions fully.

Your goal in this process, therefore, is to fully utilize the expertise at hand to weigh each feature of the policy under the "essential," "nice, if the price is right" and "strictly optional" terms of reference. This is easy if you know your objectives for this decision. Do you want insurance protection only? Then treat your insurance decision the same way you would the purchase of property or car insurance—consider the affordable protection of term insurance. But remember, when the term is up, will you be insurable again?

Do you want to accumulate a cash value as well as insure your life? Then treat this decision on the merits of its investment potential. Determine how much you could make outside of the insurance policy if you invested the difference between the term and permanent insurance premiums in a RRSP or other investment. The RRSP will likely provide you with better tax-sheltered returns as the initial contribution will result in a tax deduction and subsequent earnings are completely tax-sheltered until withdrawal. Then weigh this against the ability to withdraw cash values in your life insurance policy later, with little or no tax liability, depending on the type of policy and its earnings components.

Finally, compare costs. Let's say you decide your family would need a $500,000 insurance policy on your life so that it could earn $50,000 a year at a 10 per cent return. Compare the costs:

LIFE INSURANCE POLICY COST COMPARISON

Calculations courtesy of Lesperance Insurance and Financial Service, Winnipeg: Alan E. Lesperance, CLU.

The following is a breakdown of insurance costs and cash values for Male and Female at age 40, both nonsmokers, for a policy of $500,000. Costs are provided based on an annual premium for:

1. 10-year guaranteed renewable and convertible term.
2. Combination whole life and term.
3. Whole life with dividends.
4. Whole life with no dividends.
5. Universal life.

Rates used reflect a cross-section of the life insurance industry.

SCENARIO A: MALE AGE 40

10-Year Guaranteed Renewable and Convertible Term

Age	Annual Cost	Total Cost
40—49	$ 840.00	$ 8,600.00
50—59	2,345.00	23,450.00
60—69	6,900.00	69,000.00
70—74	13,360.00	66,800.00
	Total Cost	$167,850.00
	Total Return	Nil

Combination Whole Life and Term

Age	Annual Cost	Total Cost
40—49	$4,103.00	$41,030.00
50—59	4,103.00	41,030.00

10-Year Cost	$41,030.00	20-Year Cost	$82,060.00
10-Year Return	$30,079.00	20-Year Return	$116,134.00
Net Cost	$10,951.00	Net Gain	$34,074.00

Whole Life With Dividends (Level Premium)

Age	Annual Cost		Total Cost
40—48	$10,895.00		$87,160.00
10-Year Cost	$87,160.00	20-Year Cost	$ 87,160.00
10-Year Return	$80,839.00	20-Year Return	$196,215.00
Net Cost	$ 6,321.00	Net Gain	$109,055.00

Whole Life With No Dividends

Age	Annual Cost		Total Cost
40—49	$6,553.00		$ 65,530.00
10-Year Cost	$65,530.00	20-Year Cost	$ 65,530.00
10-Year Return	$70,715.00	20-Year Return	$134,178.00
Net Gain	$ 5,185.00	Net Gain	$ 68,648.00

Universal Life

Age	Annual Cost		Total Cost
40—49	$4,116.00		$41,160.00
50—59	4,116.00		61,740.00
10-Year Cost	$41,160.00	20-Year Cost	$ 61,740.00
10-Year Return	$28,335.00	20-Year Return	$100,524.00
Net Cost	$12,825.00	Net Gain	$ 38,784.00

SCENARIO B: FEMALE AGE 40

10-Year Guaranteed Renewable and Convertible Term

Age	Annual Cost	Total Cost
40—49	$ 795.00	$ 7,950.00
50—59	1,900.00	19,000.00
60—69	4,825.00	48,250.00
70—74	10,115.00	50,575.00
	Total Cost	$125,775.00
	Total Return	Nil

Combination Whole Life and Term

Age	Annual Cost		Total Cost
40—49	$3,142.00		$31,420.00
50—59	3,142.00		31,420.00
10-Year Cost	$31,420.00	20-Year Cost	$62,840.00
10-Year Return	$23,303.00	20-Year Return	$92,274.00
Net Cost	$ 8,117.00	Net Gain	$29,434.00

Whole Life With Dividends

Age	Annual Cost		Total Cost
40—48	$9,255.00		$74,040.00
10-Year Cost	$74,040.00	20-Year Cost	$ 74,040.00
10-Year Return	$69,175.00	20-Year Return	$171,978.00
Net Cost	$ 4,865.00	Net Gain	$ 97,938.00

Whole Life With No Dividends

Age	Annual Cost		Total Cost
40—49	$4,904.00		$49,040.00
10-Year Cost	$49,040.00	20-Year Cost	$ 49,040.00
10-Year Return	$48,971.00	20-Year return	$119,773.00
Net Cost	$ 69.00	Net Gain	$ 70,773.00

Universal Life

Age	Annual Cost		Total Cost
40—49	$3,120.00		$31,200.00
50—59	3,120.00		46,800.00
10-Year Cost	$31,200.00	20-Year Cost	$46,800.00
10-Year Return	$20,914.00	20-Year Return	$76,381.00
Net Cost	$10,286.00	Net Gain	$29,581.00

Specific Questions to Ask Your Insurance Agent about Your Policy Options

1. What is the amount of coverage I will receive for like premiums under term and permanent insurance?
2. What is the difference in the premium cost between term and permanent insurance for the same amount of coverage?
3. What are the commissions on each type of insurance contract?
4. Are there any administration fees on the policy; if so, what are they?
5. What are the future rates of the insurance policy if they are not guaranteed?
6. Are there any withdrawal fees or surrender charges?
7. What are the interest costs if I borrow against any cash surrender value?
8. Is my insurance coverage decreased if I use my cash value to pay premiums?
9. What happens to the cash value when I die?
10. What are the costs of any conversion features?
11. Is there a discount in premiums if I take more insurance?
12. How much will the policy pay if I die accidentally?
13. Do I get a discount for being a non-smoker?
14. Is the face value of my policy guaranteed?
15. How much will the accrued earnings be when I withdraw the savings component?
16. What is the grace period in which the policy is in force if premiums have not been paid, if any? What is the reinstatement period thereafter?
17. What happens if I do not repay the sums borrowed against my cash values?

Most policies have a "contestable period" of two years after the policy is taken out. If the insurer dies in this period, the company may contest the application if it suspects misstatement or concealment of facts. After this period, the policy is usually not contestable.

> **MONEY MANAGEMENT TIP 64**
>
> Choose your life insurance policy based on your needs for protection and overall goals for investment.

DISABILITY INSURANCE

I will never forget the sadness on the face of a dear friend who succumbed recently to cancer, only having reached his early forties. As he was gallantly fighting for his life, he tangled on the telephone with one bureaucracy after another to gain entitlement to disability insurance plans he had been paying into all of his lifetime. Only once did I hear discouragement in his voice: "A sick person shouldn't have to go through this," he stated, after being subjected to a cold and callous run-around in securing his Canada Pension Plan Disability Benefits.

> **MONEY MANAGEMENT TIP 65**
>
> When disaster strikes in the form of a life-threatening accident or illness, be prepared to take on the challenge of generating income, perhaps at your weakest mental state. Make sure you ask all the right questions while you are healthy.

It is quite frightening to look at the statistics surrounding the likelihood of disability. Take note:

PROBABILITY OF DISABILITY	AGE	PROBABLE LENGTH
25%	55	2.6 years
40%	45	3.2 years
50%	35	2.8 years
60%	25	2.1 years

ODDS OF LONG-TERM DISABILITY VS. DEATH

Age	Odds
27	2.7 to 1
37	3.3 to 1
42	3.5 to 1
47	2.8 to 1
52	2.2 to 1

Courtesy The Paul Revere Life Insurance Company and The Society of Actuaries.

How old will your children be when you are age 42? What needs will they have? What happens if you are disabled and your income drops dramatically? Disability insurance, if you have it, will likely only pay 60 per cent to 85 per cent of your regular income. Will your emergency fund cover the lengthy waiting periods you may have to endure?

If you become severely disabled, there are several types of disability insurance that may help you:

Canada Pension Plan Disability Insurance

Expect a waiting period of 12 to 24 months. Once you've passed through the red tape, an amount is payable to the insured as well as to dependent children. Put these amounts into Account No. 1 in the name of the child, as interest earnings accruing from this source will be taxed in the child's hands. The disability pension is taxable to the recipient, but amounts qualify as "earned income" for RRSP purposes. This means that the child benefit can be claimed by the child and be used to create unused RRSP contribution room. Retroactive payments received by the contributor may qualify for special averaging, to ensure that the entire lump sum is not subject to tax in one taxation year.

Workers' Compensation Payments

These amounts are payable only if your employer pays into the plan, and again a lengthy waiting period may be in store for you. The income is not taxable, but must be reported on your tax return for the purposes of family net income calculations that affect refundable tax credits such as the Child Tax Benefit, the GST credit and provincial tax credits.

Unemployment Insurance Payments

These amounts will likely be received the fastest out of the three government-administered plans, if you qualify. The benefits are taxable, and may be subject to repayment if your net income exceeds a certain level. This is not an option for self-employed persons. The benefits may also be repayable if Canada Pension Plan disability payments become retroactively payable to you.

Employer-Sponsored Plans

These are usually group plans that provide short-term and long-term coverage. The problem with these plans is that if your job terminates for any reason, you are usually not covered after 30 days of leaving. The premiums paid into these plans are not tax deductible. Resulting benefits will be subject to income inclusion and will qualify for RRSP earned-income purposes. If both the employer and the employee contributed to the plan, a special tax deduction can be taken in the year the benefits begin, equal to the amount of the employee-paid premiums to the plan back to 1968.

Individual Private Plans

These plans come in a variety of options. Benefits received are generally not taxable and premiums are not deductible.

With each one of these plans, find out the following:

1. What is the definition of "disabled"?
2. What circumstances are excluded from the plan?
3. How long a waiting period is there before we receive benefits?
4. How long will the benefits be paid?
5. What happens to premium payments while I'm disabled?
6. Is there inflation protection?

> **MONEY MANAGEMENT TIP 66**
>
> Claim the disability credit, available through the income tax system, for any members of your family who are severely disabled on a prolonged and continuous basis.

Finally, don't forget that a special tax credit is available through the income tax system for those who become disabled on a severe and prolonged basis. The disability credit is a lucrative one—27 per cent of $4,233 or about $1,150 a year may be taken off your taxes payable if the qualifying criteria are met. Some provinces also have additional disability credits or deductions.

The disability credit is discussed in detail in *Jacks on Tax Savings*.

UNEMPLOYMENT INSURANCE

An employee is required to pay premiums to the Unemployment Insurance Commission if he or she has worked a minimum of 15 hours a week and earned $156.00 a week. The maximum contribution for 1994 is $1,245.40 (or $3.07 per $100 weekly), based upon insurable earnings of $40,560 (or $780 a week).*

Unemployment Insurance may protect you if you lose your job. You must have worked a minimum number of weeks (12 to 20 depending on where

---

*Figures as of time of writing.

you live in Canada), you may not quit without just cause and you must declare any income you make while your are collecting benefits, which are fully taxable.

How much time you must work before collecting UIC depends on the unemployment rate in your region.

Unemployment Rate	Minimum Workweeks Required
6% and less	20 weeks
6% to 7%	19 weeks
7% to 8%	18 weeks
8% to 9%	17 weeks
9% to 10%	16 weeks
10% to 11%	15 weeks
11% to 12%	14 weeks
12% to 13%	13 weeks
over 13%	12 weeks

Source: Human Resources Development Canada. Note: those who begin a new job or re-enter the workforce after an absence of two or more years will need 20 weeks of qualifying employment, regardless of local unemployment rates.

How much will you be able to draw? The general guidelines are:
- one week of benefits for two weeks of work in the first 40 insured weeks
- one week for each week worked over 40 weeks in the next 12 weeks, plus
- two weeks of benefits for every percentage point in the unemployment rate over 4 per cent in your region
- maximum collection period is 50 weeks.

If you are self-employed, UI is simply not an option for you, so plan accordingly.

If you employ your spouse in your business, you will be required to make the required contributions if the working time or earnings levels are met. Should your spouse become unemployed, be prepared for a time-consuming fact-finding mission, conducted by the UI Commission with Revenue Canada, to verify that a bona fide contract of employment actually existed before you will see any benefits paid out. Your spouse is insurable if he or she owns less than 41 per cent of the company's voting shares.

When you employ your child, your child will be eligible for UIC premium payments of the minimum weekly dollar amounts and time requirements are met. This is provided that the amount paid is reasonable and similar to what would be paid to a non-arm's length employee. If you pay your child excessively, section 32(c) of the UI Act will exclude the earnings from being insurable. In such cases, you would indicate "exempt" on the child's T4 slip, Box 28, but beware that these situations will be audited by Revenue Canada on a regular basis.

RETIRING ALLOWANCES AND SEVERANCE PAY

Should your job be terminated, you may be in receipt of a severance package. Up to $2,000 per year of service after 1988 may be transferred to your RRSP on a tax-free basis in this instance. A further $1,500 per year of service may be eligible for this rollover for pre-1989 service in certain cases. (See *Jacks on Tax Savings*.)

CHAPTER 47 Your First Home

When you buy a home, you will generally be taking a first step towards wealth creation. This investment has the potential to provide you with:
1. Tax-exempt capital appreciation.
2. A hedge against future inflation.
3. A possibility to produce income (from rentals or a small business run out of a home office).
4. Equity that can be used to acquire other income-producing assets.

Recessionary times are among the best to get into the home buyers' market, if you can envision yourself staying in the market long enough to capitalize on an economic or inflationary upswing in the future. If housing prices are depressed in your area, consider buying, but give yourself a minimum five- to 10-year period in contemplating your capital appreciation opportunities. Liquidity may be a real problem in some areas.

If you are in the market for the short term only, and a regional economic slump is expected to persist, the best you can hope for is a maintenance of the value of your investment. You may even have to contemplate the possibility of a decrease in your equity. Renting in the short term may make some sense.

If you are in a market in which housing prices are beginning to increase, you may be considering the sale of your existing home, with the goal of "buying up."

If the regional market in your area has been heated for some time, you may want to consider selling before a decline occurs. (Remember what happened in Toronto!) The problem in these cases is always, "What do I buy next?"

Buying a home, therefore, can have real risks or downsides:

1. There is no tax deduction for interest or maintenance payments unless you produce income from your home through rentals or a home-based business.
2. If you get divorced or must move, you may not be able to sell at the right time, and therefore lose money on your original investment.
3. Mortgage renewal on a home that's too expensive for you can be devastating if interest rates rise dramatically in the period or if your income picture changes for the worst.
4. Losses on the sale of your personal residence are not tax deductible.
5. Making the wrong decisions about the level of down payment, interest rates or monthly payments can make tens of thousands of dollars of difference to you in the long term.
6. Cyclical changes in the regional marketplace can be in your favour, or not.

All of these factors should be discussed with your real estate professional, your tax professional, your lawyer and your financial institution.

HOW MUCH CAN YOU AFFORD TO PAY TOWARDS SHELTER COSTS?

According to rules followed by most financial institutions, you can afford to pay about one-third of your annual income towards total costs of home ownership, including the operating costs listed below. Therefore, if your annual income is $60,000, you can afford to spend approximately $20,000 on the costs of owning a home. This is called the "Gross Debt Service Ratio." It will usually include principal, interest and taxes.

If you have other debt, you must determine your "Total Debt Service Ratio." This would include your debt on credit cards, car loans and condo maintenance fees. A lender will want to ensure that not more than 40 per cent of your gross family income is used in servicing your total debt.

How much of a home will that buy you? That depends on how much of a down payment you have accumulated, what the prevailing interest rates are, and how long an amortization period you will opt for, as well as the costs of property taxes, insurance, and maintenance and utilities.

To get an idea of what you can afford, prepare the following worksheets.

WORKSHEET #1: GENERAL AFFORDABILITY STANDARD		
	Annual	Monthly
1. Gross Before-Tax Income	$_____	$_____
2. Gross Debt Service Ratio (30%)	$_____	$_____

Once you know how much you can spend on a home monthly, then choosing the maximum home value boils down to how much of a down payment you have, and the prevailing interest rates.

HOW MUCH OF A DOWN PAYMENT MUST YOU HAVE?

This depends upon where and how you get your mortgage. A high-ratio mortgage, approved by the Canada Mortgage and Housing Corporation (CMHC) is available to first-time home buyers for residential properties limited to certain values, depending on where you live in Canada. Such mortgages require a minimum down payment of 5 per cent of the cost of the property. For other home buyers, the minimum down payment will normally be 10 per cent.

The loan that you take will require expensive insurance, which is added to the principal. There is an application fee for the mortgage insurance, which will depend on the size of your mortgage. For example, CMHC has published the following schedule in effect at the time of writing:

Loan Size (% of property value)	Premium (% of loan)
up to 65%	0.50%
up to 75%	0.75%
up to 80%	1.25%
up to 85%	2.00%
up to 90%	2.50%

Therefore, if you have financed 90 per cent of your $85,000 home, the premium for insurance would be 2.5% × $76,500 = $1,912.50. This can be paid as a lump sum or added to your mortgage.

A conventional mortgage is one that requires a down payment of 25 per cent of the cost of the property. It will generally be the one that gives the borrower the best rate because of the level of security to the lender. It will also be to your advantage in that you would avoid the requirement to pay the mortgage insurance.

When you shop around for a mortgage (which you should do because lenders are very competitive), you should decide on a number of features to ask about beforehand.

QUESTIONS TO ASK OF YOUR MORTGAGOR
What is the best term to choose?

The term of your mortgage refers to the number of years for which a specific interest rate will be fixed. This can be 6 months or even 10 years in some cases. You might also have a 6-month or 1-year "open" term; that is, you can pay off your principle at any time in that period without incurring a penalty. An open mortgage will generally have a higher interest rate than a "closed" mortgage. Under a closed mortgage, you agree to a set payment schedule at a set interest rate for a set period, and pay a penalty if you wish to get out of your mortgage sooner. The following chart will give you an idea of the interest savings to be had if you can afford to a) reduce your amortization period, and b) increase the size of your mortgage down payment.

COMPARISON OF COSTS IN DIFFERENT AMORTIZATION PERIODS
Down payment of $25,000 on $100,000 home; 9% interest rate.
Principle borrowed: $75,000

Amortization	Monthly Payment	Total* P + I	Interest Only	Savings
25 years	$620.99	$186,297	$111,297	
15 years	753.39	135,610	60,610	$50,687 over 25 years
10 years	943.42	113,210	38,210	$73,087 over 25 years

By investing $322.43 more each month over a 10-year period, you will save $73,087 towards your financial independence.

COMPARISON OF COSTS WITH VARYING DOWN PAYMENTS
$100,000 home; 9% interest rate

Down Payment	Amortization	Monthly Payment	Total* P + I	Interest Only	Savings on Interest against $25M
$50,000	25 years	$413.99	$124,197	$ 74,197	$37,100
30,000	25 years	579.60	173,880	103,880	7,417
25,000	25 years	620.99	186,297	111,297	

*Assumption: Same interest rate throughout the amortization period.

By increasing your down payment by $25,000 up front, you'll save $37,100 in interest over 25 years. That's a 48 per cent return on your additional investment.

How big a difference will your mortgage interest rate make?

The shorter your term, the lower your interest costs will be. The trick to financing your mortgage is to get the best "average" rate over the long term. For example, if you are lucky enough to have a 6 per cent 1-year mortgage, have you been investing your interest savings to pay down the mortgage principal in the meantime? If not, are you prepared for an increase should you need to renew the mortgage at 9 per cent or higher? Those homeowners who currently hold low-interest mortgages with renewal dates coming up within five years should watch inflationary trends carefully. Are you at risk of losing your home five years from now if you can't afford a potential hike in interest rates at the time you'll be renewing?

There is no doubt that a keen eye to taking a mortgage when interest rates are low will reap substantial savings, as shown below:

COMPARISON OF COSTS WITH VARYING INTEREST RATES
$100,000 home, $25,000 down payment, $75,000 mortgage

Rate	Amortization	Monthly Payment	Total* P + I	Interest Only	Savings over 10% Rate
7%	25 years	$525.32	$157,596	$ 82,596	$43,665
8%	25 years	572.42	171,726	96,726	29,535
9%	25 years	620.99	186,297	111,297	14,964
10%	25 years	670.87	201,261	126,261	n/a

*Assumes same rate and monthly payment throughout full amortization period.

How much do I save by prepaying the principal?

Mortgages that allow you to increase your monthly payments or pay down an annual lump-sum amount to be applied directly to principal will not only help you pay off your house more quickly, but will also save you some significant amounts in interest payments.

COMPARISON OF COSTS WITH PREPAYMENTS OF PRINCIPAL
Original amortization period: 25 years on a $75,000 mortgage at 9%.
Prepayment of 20% of mortgage in each of 5 years

Year	Monthly Payment	Principal Balance*	Effective Amortization (Months)	Interest Paid in Year	Total Interest Payable on Life of Mortgage
1	$620.99	$75,000	300	$6,593	$111,297
2	620.99	59,313	166	5,226	50,364
3	620.99	45,670	107	4,110	32,595
4	620.99	33,862	70	2,817	25,536
5	620.99	23,382	45	2,204	23,309

*20 per cent prepayment plus normal amortization.

The result is that after the first five years, you have produced interest savings of $87,988 over what would have been paid under a 25-year amortization period.

Can I save money by increasing how often the financial institution gets paid?

Savings can result from changing your payment frequencies as illustrated below:

COMPARISON OF COSTS WITH INCREASING PAYMENT FREQUENCIES
$100,000 home, $75,000 mortgage at 9%. Original amortization: 25 years

Payment Frequency	Amount of Payment	Months	Total*	Interest	Savings over Monthly Payment
Monthly	$620.99	300	$186,297	$111,297	—
Bi-Weekly Accelerated	310.50	235	158,069	83,069	$28,228
Semi-Monthly	286.61	299.5	186,011	111,011	286

*Assumes same rate and monthly payment over full amortization period

It would appear that by paying your mortgage more frequently, interest savings should result. This is true but as the chart shows, they are only significant if you make the correct selection of frequency. The accelerated bi-weekly payment is calculated as the normal *monthly* payment divided by two (2), and multiplied by half the weeks in the year (26). The total annual payment made will be $8,073 ($310.50 × 26), which is higher than the normal annual payment of $7,452 ($620.99 × 12) by about one monthly payment.

The result of this is a reduction in the amortization period to 235 months or 19.58 years, and an interest savings of $28,228, because you actually make 13 monthly payments instead of 12.

With the semi-monthly payment, however, the monthly payments are calculated as the *annual* amount divided by 26 ($7,452 ÷ 26 = 286.61). The mortgagee does not make any additional payments and the slight savings realized arise from the fact that the lender receives one-half the payment half a month earlier.

> **MONEY MANAGEMENT TIP 67**
>
> The purchase of your tax-exempt principal residence should be carefully researched with your realtor and financial institution to ensure the best mortgage payment arrangements for your budget and investment goals are made.

FEATURES TO LOOK FOR IN A HOME AND THEIR COST

Once you establish your down payment and the approximate amount of monthly payments you can afford, you can start house hunting in a price range you can afford. First-time home buyers especially should be very careful about the features they seek out in their investment:

1. Location: Near work, family, schools, church, community centre?
2. Size: For today and when your family grows.
3. Type: Condo, duplex, single family, new, resale, building lot, mobile home?
4. Resale potential? How long is it taking the average home to sell in the area?
5. Trends in property taxation?
6. Upkeep? Have a qualified home inspector check out the foundation, roof, pool, eavestroughs, electrical system (how many amp service, type of wiring), basement windows, plumbing, furnace, hot water heater, fireplace, etc.

When you find a home that appears suitable, work out again the exact costs of owning that home. Be sure you can afford it—revisit your budget. For each home you look at, chart the following variables on a worksheet:

WORKSHEET #2: COST OF HOME OWNERSHIP

Location: _____
_____
_____

Price of Home:	$_____
1. Annual Principal and Interest Costs:	$_____
2. Property Taxes	$_____
3. Maintenance (1% to 2% of cost of home):	$_____
4. Utility Costs:	$_____
5. Insurance Costs:	$_____
Total Cost:	$_____
Total Cash Required:	$_____ A
Annual Income:	$_____ B
Per cent of Income: (A) divided by (B)	$_____

If you will be spending more than 35 per cent of your annual income on these basic homeownership costs, you may wish to shop around some more for a better interest rate or a less expensive house.

In summing up, it is important to determine payment amounts and terms, so that you can minimize your interest costs and maximize the opportunity for capital appreciation.

Making the Most of Your Real Estate Investment

1. Maximize your down payment.
2. Minimize your interest rates.
3. Reduce your amortization period.
4. Make principal repayments as often as possible.
5. Make your mortgage payments as frequently as possible.

To close the deal, remember that you'll need money to cover the following additional costs:
- real estate commissions plus GST thereon
- legal fees and disbursement costs and GST thereon
- fees for registration of mortgage deed
- home insurance, which could include life or disability waiver features
- land survey fees
- land transfer taxes (can be hefty!)
- connection charges for utilities
- property taxes
- GST on new homes
- interest for the time it takes to register the property at the land title office.

CHAPTER 48
Should I Buy or Rent

There are many factors that will influence your decision to buy a home or simply rent. One of these factors is cost. But others could include your lifestyle, current home prices, cost of mortgage financing, availability of vacant apartments, the likelihood of a move in the near future, marriage or divorce, the likelihood of capital appreciation in your owned property, and so on.

On a pure cash flow basis, you might likely find it cheaper to rent than to own. To find out, prepare a mini-budget:

COSTS OF RENTING

1. Rent paid annually $_____
2. Utility costs $_____
3. Insurance costs $_____
4. Parking costs $_____
5. Other costs $_____

Total operating costs $_____ A

COST OF HOME OWNERSHIP

1. Annual interest costs $_____
2. Property taxes $_____
3. Maintenance (1% to 2% of cost of home) $_____
4. Utility costs $_____
5. Insurance costs $_____

Total operating costs $_____ B

Difference in cost of owning vs. renting a home (A – B) $_____

Let's say, in the above calculation, the difference between renting and owning a home is $4,800 annually. If $400 was invested each month over a five-year period at an annual compounding rate of 8 per cent, it would yield approximately $29,391.00 on a tax-sheltered basis if invested in an RRSP. This would make a nice down payment on a home five years from now. (See Chapter 49 for details on the RRSP Home Buyer's Plan.) If you manage to buy when the market is depressed or in a slump, this down payment will go far. However, if you buy in a cycle of flattening prices, you could have difficulty with capital appreciation and liquidity.

In the meantime, if you owned rather than rented, and your home appreciated in value by at least the same amount in that five-year period, your investment could be consider to be a "forced saving" that has paid off.

If it appreciated more than your rental savings, you're ahead of the game. Then, think ahead.

> **MONEY MANAGEMENT TIP 68**
>
> Individuals with clear title homes have more security in retirement than those who spend their lifetime renting. For that reason alone, buying a home might be worth it to you.

CHAPTER 49 — Should I Contribute to My RRSP or Pay Down My Mortgage

The age-old question of which to pay first—the mortgage or the retirement fund—is best answered in relationship to time available, tax bracket and mortgage costs.

In earlier chapters, we established that contributing to an RRSP early in life will result in half the capital requirements than if you were to begin contributing later. So, even if your tax bracket is low between the ages of 18 and 28, it makes sense to contribute as much as you can to an RRSP in that period to make maximum use of your compounding time (see Chapter 44).

In Chapter 47, the point was made that the faster you pay off your mortgage, the more capital you'll have for retirement. Therefore, if you focused the next 10 years of your life (age 29 to 39) on paying down your mortgage, you could be tens of thousands of dollars ahead in interest savings. After this, you could go back to concentrating on RRSP accumulations by investing your mortgage payments. However, if you invest in your mortgage exclusively, you'll be paying if off with fewer after-tax dollars, due to the missed RRSP deductions.

> **MONEY MANAGEMENT TIP 69**
>
> Because of the cyclical nature of the real estate market, it is probably best for you to do both: contribute to the RRSP *and* pay down the mortgage.

How do you find the money? Through your tax refund, of course!

Assume you are in a 42 per cent marginal tax bracket, and you contribute your maximum contribution room to an RRSP this year (assume this is $12,000). This will save you approximately $5,040 on your taxes payable.

Now, take a look at your mortgage picture. The new money will benefit you further if applied to your mortgage. The tax savings of $5,040 equate to $420 a month. If you have a $100,000 mortgage, currently amortized over 25 years at an interest rate of 9 per cent, you would be paying approximately $828 a month. If you bumped this payment up by $420, you'd cut your amortization period by almost 15 years (monthly payments of $1,258 on a $100,000 mortgage at 9 per cent will pay it off in 10 years).

Therefore, by making your annual RRSP contribution you will do two things:

1. Accumulate tax-sheltered earnings from principal
   of $12,000 for 10 years, compounding at 9 per cent: **$198,724**

2. Save interest by taking 15 years off your mortgage
   amortization period.
   25 years × $828 × 12 months   = $248,400
   10 years × ($828 + 420 = $1248) × 12 months = $149,760
   Difference: **$ 98,640**

3. Total pre-tax accumulations by making annual RRSP
   contributions of $12,000 and investing the tax savings
   in the home mortgage over a 10-year period: **$297,364**

The numbers speak for themselves!

There are also a number of government incentives for first-time home ownership. The federal government, for example, has recently extended and renewed the provisions of the RRSP Home Buyer's Plan.

Under this plan, persons who have accumulated funds in their RRSPs may withdraw up to $20,000 of these funds without paying tax, if the money is spent on the purchase or building of a home. These withdrawals will be possible only if your RRSP is not locked in with your financial institution. If you make contributions to the fund less than 90 days before you withdraw it, your contributions may not be tax deductible. Under these rules, the part of an RRSP contribution that exceeds the balance left after withdrawal for the Home Buyer's Plan will not be deductible.

Example:
Opening balance in RRSP:	$25,000
Contribution to RRSP:	5,000
Home buyer's withdrawal (within 90 days):	20,000

Contribution will be deductible even if withdrawal is made within 90 days of contribution.

Example:
Opening balance in RRSP:	$15,000
Contribution to RRSP:	5,000
Home buyer's withdrawal (within 90 days):	20,000

No portion of the $5,000 contribution will be tax deductible, as the contribution exceeds the balance left.

Example:
Opening balance in RRSP:	$11,000
Contribution 1: outside 90-day forbidden period:	5,000
Contribution 2: within 90-day forbidden period:	5,000
Home buyer's withdrawal:	20,000
Balance in plan after withdrawal:	1,000

The $5,000 contributed outside of the 90-day period is tax deductible. So is $1,000 of the contribution made within the 90-day period. $4,000 is not deductible because it exceeds the RRSP balance after the withdrawal.

Under the current Home Buyer's Plan, you receive your tax deduction when you put the money into the RRSP for an entirely different purpose: tax-deferred retirement savings. Pulling the money out on a tax-free basis to buy a home is an incentive, but at a cost:

- of the tax-sheltered compounding time you would have had to accumulate savings within your RRSP.
- of future RRSP contributions, which might be circumvented in light of the requirement to repay at least 1/15th of your Home Buyer's withdrawal each year for 15 years. (If you miss your repayments, you'll have to add them into income, possibly paying tax at a higher bracket than when you contributed them originally.)

Depending on current market conditions and prevailing interest rates, it may be better for you to leave your RRSP savings in your plan, rent a little longer and invest the difference between your rental costs and home ownership costs for accumulation outside of an RRSP towards a down payment on your home, as calculated in Chapter 48.

These variables should be discussed with your tax advisor before you make a withdrawal under the Home Buyer's Plan.

CHAPTER 50 The Power Earning Years

Middle age. My father once told me this is the very best time of your life. If you planned it right, the years between 40 and 60 should be relatively worry free and smooth sailing. Through proper money management you find you have accomplished the following:

1. Set up an emergency fund.
2. Topped up an education fund for your children.
3. Paid off your mortgage with RRSP tax savings and other capital.

Now you're ready to party! Well, almost. What if you're not quite there yet?

GETTING BACK ON YOUR FEET

Through the recession of the late 1980s and early '90s, you lost your job or your business, you became disabled, or for some other reason, lost ground. Now, it's catch-up time. Let's say your objectives for overall annual growth in your investment portfolio is 8 per cent. Some years you've done better than that—25 per cent and more. In other years, you've lost money.

If your portfolio lost 15 per cent of its value, for example, your investments must work harder for you. Over the next five years, you'll have to average growth rates of about 11.5 per cent. Over 10 years though, that drops to about 9.75 per cent.

Therefore, the closer you are to age 60, the less absolute time you have to make up for losses. That's why you should stick to solid, steady investments that only have to work half as hard: 8 per cent average annual return is much easier to achieve than 16 per cent or more.

The following chart gives the average rate of return required if you had envisioned an average per annum growth rate (before taxes) of 10 per cent, and if you got sidetracked by losing up to 50 per cent of your portfolio. The balance left after the loss was invested for the remaining years shown.

This chart also shows why young people can afford to take more risks than the elderly.

INVESTMENT RETURNS REQUIRED TO RECOVER LOSSES
Projection: lifetime portfolio growth of 10% annually

If Portfolio Loss is the Following by the End of the First Year	Rate of Return Needed in Years					
	4	6	11	16	21	26
5%	11.90	11.13	10.57	10.38	10.28	10.23
10%	13.93	12.34	11.17	10.78	10.58	10.46
15%	16.12	13.63	11.80	11.20	10.90	10.72
20%	18.49	15.02	12.48	11.65	11.23	10.99
25%	21.07	16.51	13.21	12.13	11.59	11.27
30%	23.89	18.13	13.99	12.65	11.98	11.58
50%	38.59	26.36	17.90	15.20	13.48	13.09

*Calculations courtesy of Professor Larry A. Wood, Faculty of Management, University of Calgary

Remember that loss recovery can also be supplemented with proper tax-planning strategies. For example, if the majority of the losses arose on capital dispositions, it is possible to carry such losses forward for application against capital gains any time in your future.

If the losses resulted from investments in private small business corporation shares or debt, it is possible to use a portion of such losses against income of the current tax year, or to carry back excesses for application against income of the prior three years or next six years. In the seventh year, any excess losses remaining become capital losses.

Non-capital losses from a proprietorship, partnership or farming operation also have carry back and carry forward opportunities.

MONEY MANAGEMENT TIP 70

Reinvest your recovered taxes, found by applying prior losses, in order to rapidly make up for lost time.

OTHER KEY EVENTS

In middle age, there are a number of key lifetime events you might run into:

Probability of Disability

Between the ages of 40 and 55, you have a 25 per cent to 40 per cent chance of becoming disabled for a period of two to three years (see Chapter 46 for chart). If your earning capacity in that time is $60,000 a year, and you have no disability insurance, your net loss could be $180,000. Therefore, take good care of your health, eat well, exercise frequently, and manage stress. But if disaster strikes, adequate disability insurance will help defer at least a portion of your losses.

Separation or Divorce

Marriage breakdown (including common-law unions) will alter your financial portfolio. If this happens to you, bear in mind:

- To prepare for financial separation, do up a net worth statement at the time of divorce or separation. Your lawyer will help you with key dates, etc.
- Proceeds from the sale of the tax-exempt principal residence are tax free.
- Transfers of other capital assets will not attract a disposition at fair market value.
- RRSPs can be rolled over on a tax-free basis on marriage breakdown to an RRSP or RRIF (such transfers must be made directly). Spousal contributions may be withdrawn after separation without the usual three-year waiting period.
    Income attribution ceases upon separation or divorce if an election is made upon separation.
- The Canada Pension Plan Benefit credits accumulated by each spouse during a marriage can be split and applied for at any time. However, common-law couples must be living apart at least one year before application can be made.

In the case of assets transferring at adjusted cost base rather than fair market value, the parties can make a special election to transfer at FMV if this is beneficial (i.e., there is a loss carry forward available).

MONEY MANAGEMENT TIP 71

Consider preparing a written separation agreement, signed by both parties, in the case of marriage breakdown. It may cost much less than the non-deductible legal fees to accomplish the same result.

Legal fees paid to obtain a separation or divorce are not tax deductible. Legal fees paid to enforce the *payment terms* of a court order or written separation agreement *are* tax deductible. (Those who must go to court to enforce child visitation rights set out in their agreement may not, however, deduct those legal fees.) Tax refunds can be garnisheed and redirected to pay for outstanding support payments.

As at the time of writing, it was unclear whether child support payments made would continue to be tax deductible to the payer and taxable to the recipient, pending the appeal of the Thibeaudeau case. This case, won initially by the taxpayer in May of 1994, stated that recipients of child support should not have to report these payments as taxable income. The case was being appealed by Revenue Canada at the time of writing. Under current rules, support payments made up to one year prior to the court order or signing of a written agreement may be tax deductible if:

- the payments were made on a periodic basis
- the amounts were paid for the maintenance of the recipient and/or children of the union
- the taxpayers were living apart at the time of payment and throughout the balance of the year
- the taxpayers were separated pursuant to a divorce, judicial separation or written agreement

Note that amounts paid over and above the court-directed amounts or those specified in the written agreement will not be tax deductible.

Other tax provisions, such as the claiming of the Equivalent-to-Spouse amount, child care, Child Tax Benefit, and Goods and Services Tax Credit amounts, as well as provincial tax credits, should be reviewed with your tax practitioner when a marriage breakdown occurs.

ACQUISITION OF A SECOND RESIDENCE

If you invest in a second residence, perhaps a cottage at the lake, a condominium in the sun, or a ski chalet in Banff, your investment may bring you a taxable capital gain sometime in the future. The tax rules surrounding family residences are somewhat complicated as, over the years, the federal government has attempted to tap into the appreciating values of second residences.

This began with the year 1972, the first year in which capital gains were subject to tax in Canada. At that time, it was declared that each spouse could own one tax-exempt principal residence in their own name. Therefore, it was common that mom held the cottage and dad held the home, or vice versa. On the sale or transfer of either property, accrued gains were tax exempt.

The rules were altered in 1982 and for future years when only one tax-exempt principal residence *per family* was allowed. Instances that indicate members have left the family unit include the occasion of a child reaching age 18 or getting married, or cases where the spouses are separated.

In the case of farmers who sell farm land which includes property upon which the principal residence is located, a special election may be made to reduce a capital gain on the farm land by $1,000 plus $1,000 for each year after 1971 that the property was your principal residence. Otherwise, one-half hectare surrounding the farm house is the maximum land area that is considered to be contributing to your personal use and enjoyment.

Because of the 1981 rules, it is necessary to have a valuation of your properties, as at December 31, 1981 as well as December 31, 1971. Both your principal residence and your second or third residences should be valued. Where two properties are held, the value accrued in the ownership period 1972 to December 31, 1981 would normally not be subject to tax, but any accrued value in the property after 1981 would be, in the property that is selected to be the taxable one.

Families who own two or more family residences may designate, on a year-by-year basis, which property is their principal residence. A formal designation, using form T2091, is made in a year in which the taxable property is disposed of, or in any year that someone is granted the option to acquire the property.

No designation is required if you sell the tax-exempt principal residence only, and only one residence per year may be designated as exempt.

> **MONEY MANAGEMENT TIP 72**
> Gains on your principal residence can be received on a tax-exempt basis.

How does one choose which is the taxable residence? Well, this would generally be the one that accumulated the least value in the ownership period. The one that accrued the most value would generally be chosen as the exempt residence. However, the formula for computing the exempt portion of the gain also takes into account the length of time the property was designated a principal residence during the ownership period. In order to qualify as a designated principal residence, however, you or a member of your family must "ordinarily inhabit" the property at some time in the year.

You may also wish to look forward to future gains accrual possibilities—upon deemed disposition at death, for example. Which property will be worth more?

COMPARING TAX CONSEQUENCES WHERE ONLY ONE PROPERTY IS OWNED

Generally, ownership of a single principal residence will not result in a requirement for designation, unless that property was used for some other purpose during the ownership period (i.e., rental or business income producing). In such cases, calculate the exempt portion of the gain as follows:

1. *On actual sale or transfer.* To calculate the capital gain: take proceeds of disposition less adjusted cost base. Proceeds could be the actual sales price or, in the case of transfers, the fair market value at date of transfer. If you have only one property, the adjusted cost base is the cost of acquisition if acquired after 1971, or if acquired before 1972, the fair market value as at December 31, 1971. Add to this the cost of any additions or improvements you have made to the property since 1971.

2. *Make the Capital Gains Election for 1994.* * For the purposes of using up the $100,000 capital gains deduction, you may elect to make a deemed disposition at a value between the adjusted cost base and fair market value as at February 22, 1994. No actual disposition is required. Proceeds of disposition would be the amount between ACB and FMV, and adjusted cost base would generally be the deemed value at December 31, 1981 or, if acquired later, the actual acquisition cost plus costs of additions or improvements. The elected amount may not exceed your capital gains deduction balance.

3. *Calculate the exempt portion of the gain.* Use the following formula:

$$\frac{1 + \text{number of years property was principal residence after 1971**}}{\text{Number of tax years after 1971 that you owned the property}} \times \text{Capital Gain} = \text{Exempt Portion of Gain}$$

4. *Report the taxable portion of the gain* on Schedule 3 of the T1 General return.

5. *Calculate the "eligible portion of this gain" for the purposes of the capital gains deduction by applying the following formula.* Note that any

---

* Commentary is based on federal budget proposals and draft legislation available at time of writing.
**Include the year of acquisition and the year of sale in the calculation.

"exempt" months calculated in (3) above are not included in the equation:

$$\frac{\text{Number of months owned after 1971 and before March 1992}}{\text{Number of months owned after 1971 and before March 1994}} \times \text{Capital Gain} = \text{Eligible Gain}$$

6. Claim the eligible gain as income and on Form T657. Reduce the cumulative gains limit by the CNIL balance, if any. Minimum tax may be invoked with this claim.

PRINCIPAL RESIDENCES OWNED ON DECEMBER 31, 1981

Because of the valuation day created as of this date, capital gains accruing on second residences thereafter use the December 31, 1981 fair market value as the adjusted cost base, plus any additions or improvement made thereafter.

To calculate any exempt portion of the gain the same calculations are used, except that the "1+" year is not allowed. That is, only the actual years that the home was designated the principal residence will be allowed. Therefore, one must calculate the exemption period before 1982 separately. Form T2091, "Designation of a Principal Residence," will accomplish this task for you.

The gain calculated in the period prior to 1982 (if any) plus the gain calculated from the period after 1981 will equal the total gain. Remember that residences acquired after February 1992 will not qualify at all for the capital gains deduction.

The capital gains election, for the utilization of the remaining $100,000 Capital Gains Deduction, will also be available and calculated in a similar manner on the 1994 tax return.

These calculations are extremely complicated and should not be attempted without the help of an experienced tax practitioner. Anyone who owned more than one residence in 1994 should determine whether the pre-reporting of accrued gains for the purposes of utilizing any remaining $100,000 deduction is worthwhile.

> **MONEY MANAGEMENT TIP 73**
>
> Inheritances may be received on a fully tax-exempt basis. Earnings on subsequent investments are taxable.

INHERITANCES

During middle age, you may be in receipt of inheritances from your parents' or your spouse's parents' estates. In general, the deceased must report income received from January 1 to date of death. Several elective returns may be filed to report certain income sources such as the "value" of matured but unclipped bond coupons, dividends declared but unpaid as of the date of death, salaries, commissions and vacation pay owing but unpaid as of date of death, accounts receivable and inventories of stock, trading herds or harvested grain.

The tax consequences of the death of a taxpayer are the following, from the point of view of the beneficiary:

- Life insurance policy proceeds are not taxable. Subsequent earnings are taxable to the beneficiary.
- Interest earnings from debt securities of the deceased are claimed as follows:

  i) interest accrued from January 1 to date of death: reported by deceased

  ii) interest accrued after death: reported either by trust or beneficiaries.
- Eligible capital property that is inherited is deemed to have been sold immediately before death at four-thirds (4/3) the unamortized cost. This is relevant if you continue to carry on the business of the deceased. If not, you will be considered to have acquired a capital property equal to the deceased's proceeds of disposition.
- Land that is transferred to anyone other than the spouse is deemed to have been received at its fair market value.
- Land and eligible capital properties can be "rolled over" to the surviving spouse without immediate tax consequences.
- Business income of the deceased must be included in the final return up to the date of death. No deduction is allowed for reserves, or capital cost allowance of a sole proprietor except if a terminal loss results from the deemed disposition of property.
- A separate return may be filed for the deceased if business profits resulted in the period ending at date of death, up to the end of the normal fiscal period. Because personal amounts may be claimed again on this return, the results are usually beneficial to the estate as a whole.
- Pension benefits received up to date of death must be reported by the deceased; amounts received thereafter are usually taxable to the beneficiaries.
- Lump-sum death benefits may qualify for a tax exemption of up to $10,000. They are reported by the beneficiaries. Lump-sum death benefits from the Canada Pension Plan do not qualify for the special exemption.

- RRSP receipts: If the taxpayer died before the RRSP reached maturity, the amounts can be rolled over tax free to a surviving spouse. These amounts are called "refunds of premiums." Receipts by persons other than the spouse will be taxable to the deceased on the final return before distribution to beneficiaries. However, if there is no surviving spouse and the sums are to pass to dependent minor children, they become taxable to the child.
- The child may acquire an annuity which pays periodic amounts to age 18. This must be acquired within 60 days of the end of the year in which the money is received. If the child was dependent because of mental or physical infirmity, transfers may be made to the child's RRSP, RRIF or annuity. After 1993, it is possible to elect that some of the RRSP amounts remain taxed in the hands of the deceased if this is beneficial.
- Matured RRSPs paying periodic annuity payments will be taxed in the hands of the recipient for payments received after date of death.
- Growth in an RRSP after death can be taxed to the beneficiaries, if beneficial.
- RRIFs: The fair market value in the plan is included in the deceased's income on the final return unless the amounts pass to spouse or dependent child. The recipient of the funds is taxed only on the growth after death. If the plan passes to a spouse, the minimum amount receivable for the year of death must be reported on the final return of the deceased if the deceased was an annuitant under a RRIF. Any such minimum amount will be taxed to the beneficiary and is not available for rollover if the deceased was not receiving annuity payments.
- Capital property transferred to beneficiaries other than spouse: Any capital property owned by the deceased is considered disposed of for FMV at date of death. Capital gains or losses are recognized on the deceased's final return. The beneficiary acquires the property at the same value.
- Bequests of capital property to spouse: Non-depreciable properties are transferred at the deceased's adjusted cost base. An election can be made to transfer the property at FMV.

MONEY MANAGEMENT TIP 74

If a loved one has passed away, a special election may be made using Form T2075 to defer payment of tax on income items such as capital gains, recapture of capital cost allowance, or certain rights or things for up to nine years, if adequate security is posted with Revenue Canada.

The full utilization of special tax provisions on the final returns of the deceased will ensure that you, the beneficiary, receive more from the deceased's lifetime achievements than Revenue Canada. Be sure to get professional help.

TAX CONCERNS

Your major tax concern in the peak earning years will be how to shelter your income from the top marginal tax rates. *Diversification is generally the key.* Following are some ideas for increasing wealth in the top marginal tax brackets, they should be discussed with your tax professional.

1. *Employees.* Negotiate tax-free benefits such as discounts on merchandise, subsidized meals, uniforms and special clothing, memberships to recreational facilities such as social or athletic clubs, counselling services for mental or physical health, re-employment or retirement purposes.

    Once these items are in place, think about taxable benefits—a company car, holidays, prizes, awards, financial counselling and income tax preparation services, other consumer goods given as gifts, etc. While the value of these amounts are taxable to you, there is no real cost until you file your tax return. Invest the tax liability for the time period before your taxes are due.

    Ask your employer about alternative forms of remuneration: profit-sharing plans or share purchase plans that allow you to reap dividends or capital gains as a reward for your efforts at a reduced tax rate. Negotiate a retiring allowance and death benefit while your efforts are valued.

> **MONEY MANAGEMENT TIP 75**
>
> The negotiation of an interest-free loan from your employer is subject to tax on the benefit received. If you use that money to make investments, the taxable benefit can be deducted as a carrying charge.

2. *Investors.* Fifty per cent of interest and pensions are taxed away at the top marginal rate. Try to split income to your spouse by having second-generation earnings reinvested and taxed back to the lower earner. (See income splitting ideas in Chapter 31.) Diversification to dividend or capital-gains producing investments may reduce the tax you pay, but with a risk factor. Discuss your options with your investment dealer.

3. *Proprietors.* Employ your family members to split income legitimately. Consider incorporation for income-deferral opportunities, as well as the option to earn dividends and tax exempt capital gains on small business corporations. Discuss with your tax practitioner the advantages of creating a family trust.

PRE-RETIREMENT PLANNING

CHAPTER 51
The Challenges of Retirement

Some of us choose our time to retire; others have retirement forced upon them. Regardless of the circumstance, the event itself is a transition that is difficult for most people who have spent their lifetime gainfully occupied.

The primary challenges that face us in anticipation of our retirement are the following:

1. How long are we going to live?
2. How long will we be active and healthy?
3. What will happen to us if we become disabled?
4. How much longer can we be productive?
5. If we can't be productive, can we live on our capital?
6. What will we do when we retire?

Retirement planning, therefore, encompasses so much more than the financial aspects of your new life. It requires a revisiting of the goals and objectives you have created earlier. Together with your spouse, or perhaps on your own, you must envision your "golden years" and how you will spend them. This should be done several years before your targeted retirement date.

Statistics Canada tells us that at age 60, the average male in Canada can expect to live about 17 more years while the average female can expect to live about 21 more years. How much money will you need in that time? Let's say you budget for a bare bones minimum of $1,200 a month—over 20 years that's $288,000—a large sum for a minimum living standard. If you are active and have specific goals and objectives that include travel, gift-giving and a variety of activities, or if you become ill and need expensive part-time or full-time care, you'll need more capital.

It is important to start your money management for retirement as early as possible. Anticipate the pre-tax income you think you'll need when you retire. Certain expenses will drop off: the costs of raising children, costs of going to work or business, costs of paying for a mortgage, etc. Others may increase: medical costs, taxes, service costs, travel costs, etc.

Depending on the status of your net worth, your health and your lifestyle, you may wish to budget 60 per cent to 80 per cent of your current income for retirement. That means, if you are currently earning $48,000 a year, you'll need $28,800 to $38,400 a year to live comfortably. How much of this will come from government pensions? How much will be earned from company pensions? What will your RRSP savings bring? How hard will your capital have to work to produce the rest of what you need?

The income that you will receive in your retirement years will likely come from a variety of sources:

- government pension plans such as Old Age Security and the Canada Pension Plan
- company pension plans to which you and your employer contributed
- RRSP accumulations that will be transferred into annuities or RRIFs
- RRSPs that will be taken in lump sum investments, in the form of interest, dividends and capital gains
- business earnings
- employment earnings
- tax-exempt gains on your principal residence
- foreign pension income sources

> **MONEY MANAGEMENT TIP 76**
>
> Pre-retirement planning begins with an understanding of your financial needs and how your income sources will be taxed. Well before you retire, review your financial goals and objectives in retirement, and their tax consequences.

Prepare a net worth statement that reflects where you expect to stand financially on the day you retire. Then, prepare a budget that will anticipate new costs as well as your projected new income flows. The result will determine how much capital you must generate in the short term to enhance the quality of life you look forward to as you enter a new phase in your life.

SHOULD YOU BUDGET FOR RECEIPT OF GOVERNMENT PENSION PLANS?

Currently, if all else goes up in smoke, you can feel relatively assured that, under current tax rules, a minimum living standard will be government funded in your retirement. However, if you, like many others in Canada, feel concerned about our current government deficits and the possibility of a smaller tax-paying population base coming up behind the baby boomers, you might want to leave the CPP and OAS or other assistance out of your retirement budget plans altogether. For a high-income earner (income over $25,921), you may be subject to "Clawbacks".

Beware, high income earners may be subject to clawbacks of Old Age Security and other credits specific to seniors, such as the Age Credit. See *Jacks on Tax Savings* for details.

> **MONEY MANAGEMENT TIP 77**
>
> Consider preparing your pre-retirement budgets without counting government pensions. If you can support yourself adequately without them, you needn't worry about future tax clawbacks.

TAX DEFERRAL OPPORTUNITIES

Tax deferral in retirement is more difficult but not impossible. The taxation of annuity payments will depend on whether they are registered or non-registered. Certain registered funds—such as those originating with RRSP deposits—will bear taxable payments of both principal and earnings. They can be converted to a Registered Retirement Income Fund (RRIF) or an annuity. Non-registed funds will bear taxable payments on earnings only.

CHAPTER 52
Gifts of Charity

Death may come before retirement and old age. If you plan to leave money to your favourite charity, give yourself time to maximize your tax benefits.

> **MONEY MANAGEMENT TIP 78**
>
> Plan your charitable donations over a period of time at year end, to maximize tax savings opportunities.

The tax benefits of this credit are more immediate if you give at year end, rather than in the beginning of the new year, because the year-end gift is added to the tax return filed in the next springtime. If you give a gift in January of the new year, you'll have to wait until the following spring to reap tax benefits.

The reason that it is better for you to make donations in "instalments" during your lifetime, and over a period of years, is that charitable donations are limited to 20% of net income, unless they are Gifts to Canada or Provinces. Therefore, even if net income increases greatly in the year of death, it may be more beneficial from a tax point of view to give during your lifetime, and over a period of years.

Assume, for example that a taxpayer's net income on the final return is $150,000. He or she is limited to making a "tax deductible" charitable donation of 20 per cent of this or $30,000, even if a gift of $115,000 is given. The allowable donation of $30,000 will produce a tax credit of $34 plus $8,642 or $8,676 federally (17% of the first $200 plus 29% of the balance). With the provincial taxes and surtaxes, the gift will have reaped tax savings of approximately $13,900, based on average federal/provincial marginal tax rates.

In the year of death, amounts in excess of the 20 per cent limitation may be carried back an applied against the prior year's income, but only to the extent of the same limitation. So, if the taxpayer's income in the prior year was $56,575, he could reap tax benefits of a further $5,055 (approximate: based on an average provincial tax rate) for a total tax benefit of $18,955. This assumes, however, that charitable donations were not maximized in that year.

Had the taxpayer given $11,315 each year over the 10-year period, based on 20 per cent of a constant net income of $56,575, approximate tax savings of $5,050 or $50,500 would have resulted. Therefore, cumulative maximum donations of $113,150—based on a constant net income of $56,575—will reap tax savings of $36,600 more than a one-time contribution of $115,000. (This result assumes no carry back to prior years of excess contributions in the year of death.) While the charitable donations have no effects on the clawbacks, because they are calculated after "net income," they will have the effect of reducing taxes otherwise payable.

This example is for illustrative purposes only. Variables such as actual net income each year, provincial tax rates and changes to tax law will change the results. However, the general principle should hold true.

DONATIONS OVER 10 YEARS RATHER THAN IN YEAR OF DEATH
Desired Gift: Approximately $115,000

Net Income	Each Year for 10 Years	Year of Death
On line 236	$56,575	$150,000
Maximum donation @ 20% of net income	$11,315	$ 30,000
Credit:		
-17% x first $200	$ 34	$ 34
-29% of balance	$ 3,223	$ 8,642
Total Credits	$ 3,257	$ 8,676
Federal/Provincial Tax Savings	$ 5,050	$ 13,900
Tax Savings over 10 Years	$ 5,050 x 10 = $50,500	$ 13,900
Difference:	**$36,600**	

Speak to your tax professional about planning charitable donations to maximize your tax advantages. Also, see *Jacks on Tax Savings* for a summary of deductible charitable donations and their tax consequences.

CHAPTER 53
Seasons in the Sun

"We had joy, we had fun, we had seasons in the sun"—so goes the refrain of our cousin's—Terry Jacks—international hit song. The sunshine, somewhere south of Canada, may well be your planned destination either in retirement, or sooner.

> **MONEY MANAGEMENT TIP 79**
>
> If you plan to live in the United States for part of the year, tax implications could complicate your life.

In U.S. lingo, you could be considered to be either a "resident alien" or a "non-resident alien." If you are a non-resident alien, you will be taxed in the United States on income from U.S. sources. But, if you are a resident alien, you will be taxed in the United States, on worldwide income from all sources.

What is a "resident alien"? This is a person who meets a "substantial presence test." This person must file a U.S. Tax Return to report *world income* for the year. You have a substantial presence in the U.S. if:
1. You were in the U.S. for 183 days or more in the tax year.
2. You were in the U.S. for 31 to 182 days in the tax year, and the two prior years.*

The definition of these "days" is rather interesting; you must calculate how many days, not necessarily consecutive, you spent in the United States in each of the current and the immediately preceding two years.

THE SUBSTANTIAL PRESENCE TEST
Days present in the United States:
1. Each day in the current year counts as 1 day: _____
2. Each day in the immediately preceding year counts as one-third (1/3) day: _____
3. Each day in the second preceding year counts as one-sixth (1/6) day: _____

TOTAL _____

If the total of this calculation is more than 182 days, your are a resident alien. If it is fewer than 182 days, you are a non-resident alien.

However, you may also be considered a non-resident alien even if you meet the Substantial Presence Test.

WHAT IS A NON-RESIDENT ALIEN?

This is someone who does not meet the Substantial Presence Test or someone who does meet the Substantial Presence Test but who has a "closer connection" to Canada than the U.S. during the year and whose "tax home" is in Canada.

You have a closer connection to Canada than the U.S. if you maintain significant ties, such as:
- a permanent home in Canada
- a business in Canada
- personal belongings such as cars, furniture, clothing or jewellery in Canada
- memberships to social, political, cultural or religious organizations in Canada

---

* Starting in 1995, Canadians resident in the U.S. can expect to receive a smaller OAS/CPP cheque from Canadian authorities. It is proposed that these sources will no longer be reportable in the U.S., but that a withholding tax be introduced in the source country.

- voting jurisdictions
- a valid driver's licence

Your tax home is the location of your business or employment, regardless of where you or your family lives. If you are unemployed or do not own a business, your tax home is where you regularly live. That home must be available to you at all times.

You must advise the IRS about your "closer connection" to Canada by filing Form 8840, "Closer Connection Exception Statement." Obtain this form from the IRS in the U.S. or from the Canadian branch of the IRS at 60 Queen Street, Suite 201, Ottawa, Ontario K1P 5Y7. (Also see discussion of "resident alien" that follows.)

A non-resident alien must delineate income types:

A. Income that is connected with a trade or business in the U.S. including income from the sale or transfer of U.S. real property;

B. Income that is not connected with a trade or business in the U.S. but originates from U.S. sources—such as interest, dividends, rent or annuities.

Type A income is taxed at the same rates and using the same deductions and credits available to U.S. citizens. Type B income is taxed at a flat 30 per cent, or if a tax treaty is in place, a lower rate.

FOREIGN RENTAL INCOME

If you receive rent from your condo in, say Florida or Hawaii, you will be subject to U.S. income tax on that income. This income is subject to a flat 30 per cent rate, with no expenses or deductions allowed. However, you may elect to treat this income as business income, in which case you can take deductions and report only the net income. You will note that your management agent is required to withhold non-resident tax from gross rent and remit it directly on your behalf to the IRS. If you wish to be exempt from this non-resident withholding tax, your must give your management agent Form 4224, "Exemption From Withholding of Tax on Income Effectively Connect with the Conduct of a Trade or Business in the United States."

SALE OF REAL PROPERTY

Any gains or losses you have from the sale of U.S. property will be considered income from a U.S. trade or business. The purchaser or agent will be required to withhold 10 per cent of the gross sale price at the point of sale.

The gain or loss must then be reported on Form 1040NR, "U.S. Non-resident Alien Income Tax Return."

U.S. ESTATE TAXES

If you own real property in the United States, stock in a U.S. corporation, debt issued by a U.S. entity or an interest in a partnership doing business in the United States, an estate tax based on the fair market value of your asset at the date of death is imposed when your taxable assets are transferred.

In such cases, a special return called Form 706NA, "United States Estate Tax Return" must be filed.

Recent changes to the Canada-U.S. Tax Treaty, signed on August 31, 1994, will allow a Canadian a "unified tax credit" to exempt him or her from estate taxes on the worldwide value of assets under $600,000. Where worldwide assets exceed this amount, the percentage of such assets situated in the U.S. will be applied to the exemption threshold. For example, if the value of your worldwide assets is $1 million and 50 per cent of these are in the U.S., you would be subject to tax on 50 per cent of $600,000 or $300,000 in value. A spousal credit will also be available under a "marital rollover." Canada will allow a foreign tax credit to the estate taxes payable against foreign source income arising in the year of death. Beneficiaries may recover previously paid estate taxes all the way back to November 1988, when the new changes were introduced.

Consult a tax specialist in the area of US-Canada taxation for more information.

U.S. GAMBLING

If you win at gambling in the United States, you will also be subject to a flat tax of 30 per cent on your winnings. This amount is deducted from your jackpot before you get the cash. Be aware, beforehand, that winnings from blackjack, craps, roulette, big-6 wheel and baccarat are exempt from tax. As this income source is not taxable in Canada, there is no way to recover the foreign taxes paid.

The Internal Revenue Service (IRS) has several publications with further information:
    Publication 448, "U.S. Estate and Gift Tax Guide"
    Publication 515, "Withholding of Tax on Non-resident Aliens and Foreign Corporations"
    Publication 519, "U.S. Tax Guide for Aliens"
    Publication 527, "Residential Rental Property"
Oh, and by the way, give our regards to Broadway!

CHAPTER 54
Planning for Death

To paraphrase Benjamin Franklin, death and taxes are perhaps the only two constants we can count on from the moment of birth.

> **MONEY MANAGEMENT TIP 80**
>
> No personal financial plan can be completed without a plan for transferring assets to the next generation.

To make sure your offspring receive and keep most of what you've worked for in your lifetime, it is important to have a good understanding of how the taxman will view your final tax returns, and how effective your will distributes your assets to beneficiaries. It is also necessary to prepare a will.

Planning to pass on your assets requires yet another revisiting of your personal goals and objectives, as well as your projected net worth statement at the time of death. Wealth can be passed on during your lifetime or upon your demise. You may wish to review the following objectives in setting up your estate plan:

OBJECTIVES FOR STARTING AN ESTATE PLAN

1. Identify who your heirs are, listing their exact addresses, and communication information, as well as their relationship to you.
2. Sketch out what you wish for each of your heirs to receive.
3. Determine how much ongoing income your dependants will require.
4. List what specific capital should be used for each of the objectives you have set out for your dependants.
5. Identify a list of possible executor(s) of your affairs.
6. Identify the preferred guardians of your minor children, and how to reach them.
7. Identify how business interests are to be distributed, and to whom.
8. Identify which assets should be transferred during your lifetime, and which should be transferred only on death.

9. Identify which institutions hold your assets, including contact persons.
10. Identify your professional advisors including banker, accountant, lawyer, stockbroker, insurance agent.
11. Have a formal will drawn up and witnessed. Tell your lawyer where it is to be kept.
12. Keep all important documents in a safety deposit box and identify the location of that box to your lawyer. Also list any "secret" investments, bank accounts, location of valuables that you may have. Chances are no one will ever find them if you die without telling anyone.
13. Determine to whom you would give "Power of Attorney"—that is, the authorization to handle your affairs—in case you become severely ill or injured.
14. Find out the tax consequences of your death.
15. Review your life insurance policy holdings to cover possible onerous tax consequences upon death.
16. If you currently have a series of debts, determine and list in which order they should be paid.
17. Determine how much your executors should be paid for handling your affairs.
18. Make a list of subscriptions and other ongoing commitments that should be cancelled upon death.

MONEY MANAGEMENT TIP 81

Prepare a will—your written instructions on the distribution of your property—with the help of a lawyer.

If you do not have a will, the provincial trustee will be appointed to divide your assets. In most provinces, these will pass directly to the spouse or children. You should ask your lawyer about the specific procedures in your province of residence.

You should also enquire about "probate fees"—the proving of the validity of your will through court approval. Will your financial institution require this before assets are transferred to your beneficiaries? How much will it cost?

Once you have drawn up your will, review it periodically. Annually at tax time is a good time. This is when your annual net worth should be revised with the additional RRSP contributions or conversions, etc.

Discuss with your lawyer how changing asset mixes can be recorded without having to redo the will.

> **MONEY MANAGEMENT TIP 82**
>
> Keep all important documents, such as tax returns, books and records in good order to help your executors carry out your wishes when you are no longer here.

Finally, choose your executors carefully. These persons will have to perform important last tasks on your behalf, like disposal of your body, filing your tax returns, applying for your insurance policy proceeds, Canada Pension Plan death and survivors benefits, closing of your accounts at financial institutions and distribution of assets after all your debts have been paid off. This person should therefore have good organizational skills, good negotiating skills and be thorough and honest. The person should know when to enlist the help of a professional, such as an accountant, lawyer, real estate agent, insurance agent, etc. It would probably make sense to choose someone of your own age, who knows you and your priorities well, and someone younger, in case the other executor becomes ill or dies.

Be sure to discuss the choice of an executor thoroughly with your legal advisor.

CHAPTER 55: Self-Actualization

Personal money management begins with an analysis of our needs and desires, and the motivation to put a series of plans into place throughout our lifetime to meet those needs.

Once we have satisfied our primary needs—food, clothing, shelter—an understanding of what motivates us to act further in planning our financial destiny is necessary.

Anyone who took an introductory psychology course may remember Maslow's "Hierarchy of Needs." This gentleman identified "self-actualization" as the highest state of human needs.

A person who has achieved "self-actualization" has been successful in meeting basic human needs and is, as a result, satisfied with life. Such persons are more sure of themselves and others. They are unafraid to be spontaneous and enjoy what this world has to offer: simple things, like the joy of friendship, and the beauty of nature. In short, the self-actualized individual is free of the pursuit of basic needs. This person can enjoy the world around them, without fearing uncertainty in the future.

Your personal financial plan can help you achieve self-actualization. As you have read in this book, you have participated in custom-designing your own personal money management plan, as one that is goal- and action-oriented. This plan must change several times throughout your lifetime to meet your changing life cycles. It must, therefore, be revisited and remodelled several times. It can be as detailed or simple as you choose to make it. Used to its fullest potential, a personal money management plan can be documented and passed on to the next generation as an educational tool. At the very least, it can be used as a guideline in making key financial decisions that will determine whether your family's basic needs are met.

If we were to summarize the chronological steps that should be taken in our lifetime to ensure the meeting of needs and desires, it might look like this:

MONEY MANAGEMENT TIP 83

Basic Guidelines for Meeting Financial Needs from Birth to Death:
1. Learn how to keep financial statements for your family: net worth, cash flow, budget, bank reconciliation.
2. Set goals and objectives for your personal financial plans.
3. Save as much money as possible as early in life as possible, keeping an eagle eye on rates of return.
4. Be productive at an early age, enhancing your work ethic throughout your lifetime.
5. Take care of your physical and mental health.
6. Maximize your exposure to educational opportunities that result in thinking and analytical skills as well as experience-based technical and entrepreneurial skills.
7. Choose your mate with care. A lifelong partnership needs financial parameters.
8. If at all possible, plan to have children when you are ready, financially, to take care of them to adulthood.

9. Contribute to your RRSP regularly and as early in life as possible.
10. Acquire a tax-exempt personal residence.
11. Protect yourself and your family from calamities beyond your control by having the right kind of insurance.
12. Know your investment options so that you can control the level of risk and reward you desire.
13. Plan for an orderly disposition of your assets to your dependants in the event of your timely, or untimely, demise.
14. Keep on top of the changing tax rules throughout your lifetime.
15. Revisit your goals and objectives every time you enter a new life cycle.
16. You can't know everything, so enlist the help of a professional team dedicated to your goals.
17. Strive for self-actualization—the satisfaction that comes with having met all of your basic needs.

Managing your money will be a lifelong affair. Take action and watch it grow. But remember that your money is only a tool that will help you in your quest for satisfaction.

In the words of Henry Ford: "If money is your hope for independence, you will never have it. The only real security that a person can have in this world is a reserve of knowledge, experience and ability."

Don't forget, life is short. Take the time to smell the roses along your road to financial independence.

I hope the information contained in this book will help you think about money management issues, ask the right questions of your financial management team and gain peace of mind.